# 1

## History of the Port

*History is a cruel stepmother, and when
it retaliates, it stops at nothing.*
                                V.I. Lenin

*History is more or less bunk.*
                        Henry Ford

In the sphere of North Atlantic shipping, nature was fairly equitable in dispens-
ing her favors among the various North American ports from the Maritimes to
Hatteras. No one port enjoyed incomparable advantages or suffered insurmountable handicaps; all were placed on a relatively equal footing on a coastline predestined for intense competition.

While Boston is blessed with one of the finest harbors in the world and is
the nearest American port to northern Europe, favorable physical characteristics
abounded elsewhere along the newly settled seaboard. The Canadian Maritimes
were nearer to both Europe and the rich fishing ground of the Grand Banks.
Maine's coastline presented numerous and equally fine harbors. Chesapeake Bay
was not only more centrally located but offered a milder climate and adjacent
agricultural wealth. Boston, furthermore, enjoyed no great tributary — such as
the St. Lawrence, the Hudson, or the Delaware to guarantee it a natural concentration of goods to and from the interior. Finally, its hinterland was confined by
a foreign presence to the north and the Berkshire Mountains to the west and produced no staple to compare with those of the middle and southern colonies. In
fact, if any North Atlantic port had an edge in natural potential, it was New
York, Boston's ultimate nemesis; but it was over a century before the southern
rival was able to capitalize upon its geographic and physical assets and emerge
from behind Boston's shadow.

Necessity and ingenuity determined the initial maritime orientation of Massachusetts, and exigencies rather than natural advantages determined the early
preeminence of the Port of Boston. Though the first settlers of the Massachusetts Bay Colony intended to till the land in traditional English fashion, the in-
hospitable soil was incapable of meeting the increasing food demands of continued immigration, and soon the marginal agricultural economy was perilously
strained. The threatened and resourceful newcomers instinctively turned seaward to an environment familiar to most of them. Fishing the oceans proved to
be a much more assured means of survival than had farming the land. Furthermore, the "sacred cod," so bountiful in nearby coastal waters, provided not only

1

a much needed staple but an attractive export as well. The ocean offered both its produce and the means to market it. This was not lost on the pragmatic colonists who saw that the profits of distributing even their limited resources could contribute as much if not more to a stable economy than actual production. Before long, a seaborne trade flourished among the settlements and with the local Indians. Distant coastal commerce with Virginia, Maryland, the Dutch settlements on Manhattan and Long Island, and the French colonies in Canada quickly followed. Fish, liquor, and linen cloth were the principal exports, while corn, tobacco, sugar, brass pieces, beaver skins, and sheep were the major imports.

Good Puritan business sense also indicated that local ship construction would be both a convenient adjunct to this developing commerce and enhance its profitability by reducing reliance on outside vessels. It was an easy transition from building boats for the local fisheries to building ships for the maritime trades. In 1631, John Winthrop's *Blessing of the Bay,* the first sizable ship built in Massachusetts, was launched at Medford and signaled the birth of a famed and lucrative shipbuilding tradition. With increased maritime activity, waterfront facilities were improved and a gradual filling of marshes and swamps pushed Boston's watermark out to the deeper waters of the harbor. Bounties were offered to public spirited citizens who would extend the shoreline, and by the early 1630s the first town dock was constructed. The interdependent pursuits of fishing, shipbuilding, and seaborne commerce were already well on their way to becoming the dominant colonial industries.

From these early limited trade patterns, Massachusetts developed a true maritime commerce by the middle of the century. The Massachusetts Shipping Register of the time outlines the impressive extent of the new colony's shipping activities. In 1698, Boston alone could claim 124 vessels totalling 6443 tons, making it far and away the leading shipping center in the mainland colonies.[1] In fact, historian Bernard Bailyn, utilizing these registers and other sources of data, found that a realistic assessment of this fleet in contemporary terms necessitated a comparison with England rather than with any other colonial port.

In discussing the shipping of Massachusetts and its metropolis, then, we are dealing with one of the major maritime centers of the Atlantic world. In magnitude its shipping was easily the most important in America; its equivalent was the ancient port of Bristol, second only to London in the British Isles.[2]

Several varied factors contributed to Boston's success. The financial base of this rapid commercial rise was not supplied by a gradual expansion of native investments but rather by a sudden infusion of outside capital.[3] In the 1640s, numerous London merchants and tradesmen funneled large capital investments into local enterprises through settlers who were either relatives or social associates. After this initial stimulus, colonial initiative expedited both the accelerated growth of shipping and the transfer of control into local hands. By the end of the century, not only did the industrious colonists to a great extent own their own fleet and shipyards, but were already looking abroad, especially to England, to extend the utilization of both resources. Two other external circumstances significantly influenced this broadening of colonial trade. The English Navigation Act of 1651 restricting the colonial carrying trade to English and colonial vessels, eliminated any competition from Dutch New Amsterdam and lent added impetus to Massachusetts' maritime industries. Secondly, civil war in England aggravated the scarcity of foreign commodities reaching Massachusetts and led to expanded colonial trade routes in an effort to establish alternate sources in new and widely dispersed ports in the New World. Contributing to the evolution of distant commerce was the fact that the character of the limited local exports precluded an effective transatlantic trade with the mother country, the colony's most obvious trading partner. Well supplied with fish, beef, and lumber, England afforded little market for the only staples Massachusetts could provide and, thus, exposed an export deficiency that was to plague Boston forever. At the time, the Port was more fortunate than it would be later; placed in such a prejudiced position, the colony required a new and more receptive marketplace and soon discovered one in the West Indies.

The plantation economy of the "sugar islands" had to import every necessity of life, and readily absorbed New England offerings, especially lumber, provisions, and dried fish. Ambitious Boston merchants soon devised an additional, triangular trade route to complement this direct traffic. Local rum was carried to the west coast of Africa where it was bartered for slaves; the slaves, in turn, were transported across the Atlantic and exchanged for West Indian molasses; once the molasses was returned to Boston, the "Golden Triangle" was closed and New England distilleries had the basic ingredient for more rum. In this circuitous but successful fashion, the Massachusetts and Rhode Island rum industry was able very profitably to meet the burgeoning domestic demand for its product. Furthermore, since sales to the islands exceeded purchases, this scheme was essential to counter the imbalance of imports over exports that had already reared its nasty head in trade with England. Through bills of exchange, specie, and native produce obtained in the islands, Boston shipmasters were able to procure from other regions the cargoes needed for a more equalized British trade. Soon the West Indies trade became the keystone of Massachusetts' maritime commerce and was largely responsible for the steady growth of the Port of Boston. By the late seventeenth century, over 60 percent of the traffic in the harbor was working this route. A trade had been established that was to last over 250 years — Boston had surely become "the mart town of the West Indies."

Boston's expanding trade was not limited to the West Indies. Although this route continued to be the most profitable and engaged more than one-half of the Port's foreign shipping up to the Revolution, the range and diversity of Boston's commerce was also increasing elsewhere. Trade begun in the late seventeenth century flourished in the prosperity that followed the Peace of Utrecht in 1713. Reliance upon England for imports decreased and a wide variety of goods was brought in from European, Mediterranean, and South American ports. From 1714 to 1717, some 1,267 vessels, totaling 63,000 tons and employing 8,000 to 9,000 seamen, sailed from Boston for distant foreign ports.[4]

Behind this trade expansion was a growing export base that consisted of a variety of goods including dried codfish, which by 1700 had become the mainstay of Boston's outbound cargoes. Also composing this melange were whalebone, whale and cod oil, pickled mackerel and shad, masts, boards, staves, shingles, potash, horses and livestock, pickled beef and pork, beeswax, and other sundries. On the liquid side of the ledger, in 1773, New England as a whole exported 911,000 gallons of rum — 419,000 gallons of which went to Africa, 361,000 gallons to Quebec, and 111,000 gallons to Newfoundland.[5]

Supplementing this foreign trade, numerous small vessels out of Boston developed a varied and prosperous coastal trade with the other North American coastal colonies. This "mosquito fleet" exchanged a variety of local goods for tobacco, grains, naval stores, and beaver and seal skins. With rapid development, Boston's coastwise traffic entailed about 800 voyages a year by the mid-1700s.

As a result of its expanding seaborne commerce, Boston remained the largest town in the English colonies and the major trade center in North America until the middle of the eighteenth century. Between 1699 and 1714, 1,057 vessels totaling 59,350 tons were registered in Boston. [6] Even though these figures must be qualified since they do not reflect the rapid contemporary replacement rate or subsequent reregistration at a later date, they were remarkable for the time. The pace of shipbuilding in Massachusetts during this period was equally impressive. Between 1674 and 1714, 1,257 vessels totaling 75,267 tons were built in the colony, with Boston accounting for 437 of them.[7] More and more vessels were being built for external markets, particularly England and other British possessions. Figures from the Massachusetts Register of Shipping for this time also reveal that shipping and shipbuilding were increasingly concentrated in Boston, in line with the traditional maritime tendency. Not only the largest number of vessels but also the largest vessels in the colony concentrated in the major port; between 1711 and 1714, 84.6 percent of Massachusetts' vessels — representing 90.0 percent of the total tonnage — were held by Boston.[8]

Though this increasing centralization limited the aspirations of smaller New England ports and producers — such as New Haven, Salem, and Scituate — it attested to the marked economic maturity Boston had attained as a result of its maritime endeavors. As Professor Bailyn's study indicates, maritime enterprises were the backbone of "a critical stage in the process by which the struggling, formless frontier economy of seventeenth-century America matured into the orderly commercial world of the eighteenth century."[9] Within this commercial ambiance, merchants ruled the social and political life of the colonial metropolis. In fact, the character and extent of the shipping industry in Massachusetts at this time invites historical speculation on its diffuse social and political ramifications. Though a familiar "merchant aristocracy" was developing at this time, shipping represented one of the most democratic endeavors in the colony; in the first decade of the 1700s, practically one of every three adult males in Boston enjoyed some degree of ownership in at least one oceangoing vessel.[10] This extent of participation only underlies the dominant role of maritime commerce throughout the entire fabric of life in colonial Boston.

Several factors were responsible for Boston's supremacy after necessity, external impetus, and local initiative had irrevocably directed it seaward. In this early stage, the Port was able to draw on local resources for export products that were in demand in many domestic and foreign markets, though not necessarily England. Secondly, Boston had evolved as the major distribution center for the North American colonies and, as such, served an area much larger than its immediate hinterland, which by itself was the most populous on the continent. Finally, Boston experienced the luxury of no significant competition from the other American North Atlantic ports. Unfortunately, as the relative marketability and volume of New England's export media fell and competition from other ports reduced Boston's service area, the Massachusetts' "metropolis" would be profoundly affected.

Boston's preeminence did not remain so secure for much longer. In 1749, Philadelphia burst upon the scene with the sudden explosion of its maritime trade and successfully maintained a small commercial lead over Boston for the rest of the century. More important for Boston's long-range prospects, however, was the awakening of maritime impulses in New York. Frustrated with seeing much of its commerce and financial affairs funneled through its northern neighbor, New York imposed duties on British goods routed through Boston and, by 1749, had developed a trade with England exceeding that of all of New England combined.[11] By 1770, competition had altered the American shipping picture to reveal Philadelphia leading Boston in arrivals with 47,000 tons to 38,000, while Charleston and New York ran very close with 27,000 and 25,000 tons respectively.[12] Not only had Boston lost its earlier dominance, but New York had established a viable rivalry that held ominous portents for the future.

Though Boston became the headquarters of the American Revolution largely because the policies of George III threatened her maritime interests, the war itself destroyed the city's commerce and industry. Hardest hit of all American ports by the conflict, Boston was further handicapped by the subsequent British trade regulations which specifically and vindictively discriminated against New England exports of lumber and fish to the West Indies. The Port's competitive position suffered; and it was New York, not Boston, that was finally able to wrest the commercial lead from Philadelphia in 1797. In 1789, however, the first Congress had adopted customs regulations designed to make Boston the leading port of the United States. Once again, despite a relative loss of stature, maritime ascendancy rescued the local economy and, as Boston's commerce expanded, both the seaboard and the interior entered a period of prosperity.

Expansion was not limited to the familiar European and coastal trades. Hampered by the new trade restrictions in the West Indies, Boston turned to newer and safer markets. An eastern Mediterranean trade in fruit, oil, and wine proved profitable and opened a larger number of ports to Boston vessels. More important, by the early nineteenth century a new Baltic trade had become extremely lucrative for Boston merchants, with Russian hemp, iron, and duck linen exchanged for New England rum, Virginia flour and tobacco, and imported tea and coffee. Surpassing even the profitable Russian business, however, was the China trade begun in 1793. Although the pattern was again unfolding to reveal Boston's weakness — that of lacking a suitable export medium — Yankee inventiveness cultivated another prosperous, indirect trade scheme for the Far East. Local ships carried cutlery, ironware, clothing, blankets, beads, and molasses to the Pacific Northwest where they were bartered with the Indians for sea otter furs. These beautiful black furs, prized in the Orient, were in turn shipped to China, where they were traded for chinaware, sugar, curios, and tea. By the early 1800s, Boston vessels dominated the China trade with nearly nine-tenths of the market.

Although surpassed by New York and Philadelphia in total tonnage, Boston enjoyed unprecedented prosperity at the start of the nineteenth century. Much of this resulted from the increased demand for American provisions precipitated by the Napoleonic Wars in Europe. Boston vessels were the chief carriers of these foodstuffs and by 1807 Massachusetts was the largest shipowning state in the Union. Massachusetts' commercial strength had come to rest on a complex interlocking system of maritime industries, none of which were self-sufficient. Protected by the policies of the federal government, this imposing economic structure was founded upon, among other components, a successful fishery; a preeminent shipbuilding industry; a vast, proven fleet; venturesome merchants; and clever traders. Profits were based not so much on Massachusetts' limited exports, but rather on Boston's status as an emporium of world trade. Even by this time, Boston had little to directly offer the major trade routes. Yankee ingenuity, skillful trading, and concocting delicate, multicornered trade patterns to sustain a major distribution role for the Port could overcome this handicap only temporarily. Extensive and prosperous as this commercial edifice was, it proved peculiarly vulnerable.

The embargo and blockade of the War of 1812 almost destroyed Massachusetts' maritime commerce. It was asserted, "with some plausibility that [President] Jefferson's ultimate object was to destroy New England's wealth and power."[13] This xenophobia proved exaggerated, however, and prosperity did return after the Treaty of Ghent, due in part to favorable treatment from the British in appreciation of New England's consistent opposition to "Mr. Madison's War." Nonetheless, the conflict materially altered the economic structure of Massachusetts and began a new era in Boston's maritime history. Samuel

Eliot Morison has concisely described this next phase: "A toilsome advance in the eighteen-twenties was followed by perceptible speeding-up in the thirties, full-tide prosperity in the forties, and a glorious culmination in the fifties, with the clipper ship."[14]

In the peaceful era following the defeat of Napoleon and the Congress of Vienna, Europe recovered its own carrying trade and became less reliant on American produce. Boston subsequently lost much of its export traffic. Moreover, a westward migration in the United States left Massachusetts, isolated in the northeastern extremity of the country, more remote from the shifting center of population, consumption, and agricultural production. As conduits between Europe and the West, ports nearer the growing interior — such as Philadelphia, Baltimore, and New Orleans — threatened Boston's commercial base. Most important, however, New York consolidated its hitherto tentative position as the leading United States port on the North Atlantic and began to present insurmountable competition to Boston.

In 1825, the Erie Canal was opened and tapped the interior west of the Alleghenies for traffic through the port of New York. The canal extended from Albany to Buffalo and linked the Hudson River with Lake Erie. It established New York as the entrepôt of western commerce and was instrumental in creating an agricultural boom in the West. Despite popular misconception, the great physical advantage afforded by "Clinton's Ditch" was not the primary factor in ensuring New York's preeminence; as Robert Albion has clearly shown in his study of the port, the canal only made obvious the great strides New York had made since the War of 1812, cumulatively guaranteeing it the exclusive status of America's major commercial emporium.[15] New York's first competitive break came by good fortune when the British decided to use the port for "dumping" the manufactures that had accumulated under the embargo of the war. Subsequently, New York took the initiative on two counts to ensure the continued flow of these goods and the commercial benefits they generated. In 1817, the state passed favorable auction laws to attract more buyers; more importantly, the first regularly scheduled ocean liner service to Liverpool, the famous Black Ball Line, was inaugurated early the next year. New York was equally aggressive and successful in diverting the cotton trade between England and the southern ports through its own harbor. Though of often dubious propriety, this maneuver captured the lucrative "Cotton Triangle" for New York and, thus, allowed it to collect tolls on the nation's most abundant export as well as providing ample eastbound cargoes for Liverpool. Hence, while the Erie Canal was important in opening up a greater area for import distribution through New York, it was only one contribution to the progress the port had made over the previous ten years. Even by 1823, the situation was apparent when the New England Society toasted "The City of New York — the emporium of America; commerce her glory, rivalship hopeless."

Boston's future, on the other hand, was looking dim as the Port began to face the dire consequences of overwhelming competition and an inexorable attrition of its hinterland. Boston experienced only frustration in its three attempts to establish ocean-packet service due to a shortage of eastbound cargoes; this was a crucial failure. The packets offered fast and regular service that expedited freight forwarding and minimized unproductive delays; this made it easier and usually quicker to distribute transatlantic shipments through New York to other American ports. Once habits formed around these benefits, New York was able to reap profits from traffic that previously would never have used the port. New York was gradually monopolizing American trade with western European ports and appropriating the entire nation for its hinterland. The consequent reduction in Boston's sphere of influence inspired the first of many historical complaints by port interests that the New York lines were using lower than normal rates to lure away local import business.[16] "A sullen pessimism was the prevailing attitude on State Street. The decline of Boston to a fourth-rate seaport . . . [was] confidently predicted."[17] Though this prognosis eventually proved prophetic, at the time, just when the Port most needed a stronger export base, it was granted a wonderous respite.

During the recent war, the manufactures the young nation had traditionally acquired from England were cut off. This instigated some shrewd, prescient Yankees to divert capital into industry. In 1814, the first complete cotton factory in the United States was established at Waltham, Massachusetts. New Englanders found in the factory the assured wealth the soil had initially denied them. A wave of industrialization followed. Textile and paper mills, iron foundries, tanneries, and shoe factories soon turned Lowell, Lawrence, Chicopee, and Manchester into manufacturing cities. By 1840, Massachusetts was predominantly a manufacturing state and Boston's maritime prosperity depended on these new enterprises.

Port activity gradually became oriented around the functional priorities of supplying food for the region's growing population and fuel and raw materials for its growing industries. Boston's coastwise trade kept pace with this increasing reliance on imports. Cotton and coal were the necessary ingredients for the new economy. The Port's cotton imports from the South leaped from 25,000 bales in 1832 to 270,000 in 1849.[18] Anthracite coal imports from Philadelphia for industries, stoves, and furnaces went from 63,000 tons in 1830 to more than a million in 1850.[19] These two commodities account for America's coastal tonnage exceeding its foreign tonnage for the first time in 1831 and the continuance of this trend despite the increasing rivalry that the railroads were offering seaborne transport.

New England sent out everything its limited export base would allow in exchange for these domestic receipts. Lumber, apples, and fish were sent to Philadelphia and Norfolk for coal; and boots, shoes, woven cotton, and granite were transacted for Southern corn and cotton. Yankee imagination even concocted means of loading ships with ice and sailing it to Dixie for mint juleps. This burgeoning domestic trade nearly doubled Boston's coastwise shipping from 5000 arrivals and departures in 1830 to 9300 in 1848.[20]

Until the Civil War, Boston's foreign commerce also expanded, but at a slower rate. This increment also resulted from the need for imported raw materials and food. The Northwest fur trade declined as an increasing amount of the China trade whent to New York. The Port's Mediterranean trade increased tremendously, however. Exporting cotton and rum, Boston led New York in imports of wine and fruit until 1850. Industrial demands sent local ships along new trade routes to the Baltic, exchanging western grains and manufactured goods for Swedish steel and Russian hemp. A South American trade grew to be as important for Massachusetts' commerce as the West Indies trade of colonial days. From Buenos Aires and Montevideo, hides were hauled for New England tanneries and shoe factories along with Brazilian coffee and River Plate wool for local looms. For these goods, Boston shipped lumber, ice, boots, cotton and woolen cloth, shovels, and machines. Even the prestigious East-India trade supplied New England with needed raw materials such as buffalo hides, indigo, linseed, shellac, and salt peter. All of these imports were destined for the New England area except for gunnysacks for western corn growers and gunnycloth for southern cotton growers. In 1857, there were 3,012 foreign arrivals amounting to 714,821 tons in Boston.[21]

Despite the prosperity this volume of foreign trade brought to Boston, an important fact cannot be overlooked. Though the export of local manufactured goods increased, at no time during the 1850s did Boston's total exports amount to even one-half of its imports from the established trade routes. Industrialization was an illusory antidote for New England's export deficiency. The vast majority of local manufactured goods were absorbed by the domestic market. Furthermore, the shoes, boots, and textiles of New England's factories, while of high value, were of small bulk. When shipping was gradually wrested from the control of local merchants, the inability of the products of local enterprises to fill outgoing ship bottoms became a critical handicap. In order to attract and maintain the regular and frequent service so vital to a port, a somewhat balanced volume of trade is a prerequisite. Industrialization would not prove the source of an export medium adequate for this function. Boston came to rely not only on external raw materials but also on nonindigenous bulk exports from outside its immediate hinterland to sustain an essential ocean traffic. This festering dilemma was now clearly exposing the Port's singularly insecure maritime foundation.

The clipper ship era, beginning in 1850, was considered by many as the romantic and commercial apogee of Massachusetts' maritime history. In retrospect, it appears more as a miscalculated investment. Though a need was long recognized in the China tea trade for faster vessels, the California gold rush of 1848 gave the real impetus to build and sail ships which sacrificed cargo space for maximum speed. The premium placed on the rapid transport of men and provisions of all sorts to San Francisco resulted in some of the fastest sailing vessels ever built, with Donald McKay creating such legendary masterpieces of oak, hemp, and canvas as the *Sovereign of the Seas* and the *Flying Cloud*. The clipper era was shortlived, however. San Francisco became so flooded with goods that freight rates dropped to a barely remunerative level. Clipper ships became too costly to operate even in shorter coastal and transatlantic voyages, and, sadly, none were built after 1855. The passing of the clipper can be said to have ended Boston's maritime history as distinct from the nation's as a whole.

At the end of the clipper era, Boston was a metropolis of refinement and wealth, the richest city for its size in the world. Despite this prosperity, Boston was rapidly losing ground to New York in maritime commerce. In the first half of the nineteenth century, Boston concluded the process of concentration that had been established earlier; in her struggle to compete with New York, she absorbed the commerce and shipping of every other Massachusetts seaport including famed Gloucester, Newburyport, and Salem. Concurrently, however, the same process on the national scale was concentrating much greater water-borne commerce in New York. In 1845, New York's fleet surpassed that of Massachusetts. And, by 1860, New York could boast of having over three times as many tons of shipping as Boston. Though, in 1857, Boston had 2842 foreign arrivals from the major trade routes to 2990 for New York, the figure disguises the fact that 1913 of Boston's arrivals were small Nova Scotian schooners.[22] Table 1-1 clearly indicates the relative status of the major North Atlantic ports and the absolute predominance of New York during the period prior to the Civil War.

New York was emerging as one of the great international ports because it was able to corner the distribution of imports and exports for a national market area. Self-reinforcing concentration was affording it the commerce of a great

Table 1-1
Relative Maritime Activity of Principal North Atlantic Ports, 1821-1860
(percentage of national total for the period)

| | Imports (by state) | Exports (by state) | Registered tonnage | Registered Steam Tonnage (1828-1860) | Shipbuilding Tonnage (1833-1860) |
|---|---|---|---|---|---|
| New York | 60.3 | 32.9 | 26.8 | 75.9 | 15.4 |
| Boston | 15.7 | 8.4 | 16.9 | .7 | 9.4 |
| Philadelphia | 7.5 | 3.6 | 4.7 | – | 4.9 |
| Baltimore | 3.2 | 3.7 | 5.1 | .1 | 4.0 |

*Source:* R.G. Albion with Jennie Barnes Pope, *The Rise of the Port of New York, 1815-1860* (New York: Charles Scribners' Sons 1939), appendix I, p. 389. Copyright 1939 Charles Scribners' Sons. (Figures compiled from annual Reports on Commerce and Navigation.)

# Preface

"Outside of the Eighteenth Amendment, port development is about as dry a subject as you can think of." So would Alfred E. Smith begin meetings with business and civic groups back in 1921 when he was a commissioner of the newly formed Port of New York Authority. With theatrical, as well as political flair, however, he would belie his own words and impress upon his audience the vitality, complexity, and utility of a seaport. The same approach could be adapted to any port that is, or once was, a major commercial center.

Most New Englanders are curiously conscious and proud of their legacy of a unique maritime heritage. Yet for most, this manifests itself in regattas off Marblehead or faded daguerreotypes of a long removed romantic era. Few in Massachusetts, or even in the metropolitan Boston area, however, understand their Port's past, and fewer still appreciate its present contributions and sympathize with its struggles and problematic future. Ask a Bostonian about the seaport and he will just nostalgically sigh that it is not what it used to be. Only an extensive and exclusive waterfront rehabilitation effort has sustained genuine popular interest based on a local preoccupation for a more attractive, stimulating, and urbane environment. These residential, recreational, and commercial redevelopment plans, however, disregard the more mundane maritime activities and offer nothing but a cosmetic for the real business of the seaport. Nonetheless, local residents really cannot be faulted for a lack of avid concern about railroad differentials, container cranes, demmurage charges, and pension funds. Establishing even a modest perspective on the past, present, and future of the Port of Boston is a more complicated task than meets the eye or appeals to the casual observer.

Ports by nature are much more complex commercially, politically, and socially than other transportation units, such as railroad terminals, airports, and truck depots. A broad and diversified perspective is necessary to sketch the rise or demise and current character of any significant seaport, for only against such a backdrop can the intricate interplay of shipping dynamics be appreciated. Traditionally, prevailing patterns of distribution, competition, and concentration have dominated the main currents of maritime development and prescribed the fates of participating individuals and ports. As a port's significance rises and its sphere of interest widens, moreover, it is inevitably affected more and more by national, and even international, trends that just by those of a local or regional nature. There is ample historic evidence of the seemingly inexorable economic logic underlying these critical maritime patterns of distribution, competition, and concentration. Tyre, Genoa, and Boston were, in turn, the beneficiaries and victims of the same general forces that today funnel prosperity to New York and Rotterdam.

These inner dynamics of the shipping industry are neither peculiarly maritime nor particularly abstruse in their economic logic. Basic production and consumption limitations dictate that no port can realize genuine and lasting importance exclusively on the merits of its own local products for exports and its own local needs for imports. Hence, servicing the distribution of cargoes to and from a much larger area has always been a prerequisite for success and only a large scale entrepôt can enjoy the dual status of major international seaport and world financial center. Given this incentive, efforts among rival ports to expand or monopolize both inland service areas and ocean trade routes has traditionally made shipping an intensely competitive enterprise, especially in commercially active regions with several alternative ports. A natural corollary to this competition for finite market resources has been an unusually strong tendency in the maritime industry toward concentration. This strong predisposition towards centralization is a direct reflection of the inherent commercial and logistical advantages of utilizing a minimum of strategically situated distribution points.

Further complicating an analysis of Boston or any other seaport is the diversity of elements underlying these dominant patterns. Though many are quick to explain all in geographic terms, simple geography has rarely been the sole arbiter of maritime distribution contests. Furthermore, commercial and economic developments, other obvious explanations, are often not enough to complete the picture; constant consideration must also be given to demographic, social, and political developments. In truth, a port's evolution can neither be chronicled nor anticipated without recourse to even more elusive factors, such as the timing and effectiveness of local initiative; conditions and decisions external to a port; the strength of customary attitudes and practices; and, inevitably, chance. Alone or in combination, these important variables usually play a decisive role in the ultimate exploitation or frustration of the intrinsic natural endowments of any seaport.

Given these intricacies of the shipping industry, if the saga of the Port of Boston were a curriculum offering in local schools, it would effectively span many academic disciplines. It would entail not only 300 years of the seaport's evolution, but also the historical development of the region and even the nation. Its economic concepts would be vividly presented against the backdrop of international commerce. It would shed light upon various approaches — traditional and innovative, successful and unsuccessful — of public administration and business management. It could focus on governmental goals and mechanisms and political processes and infighting. It could highlight the necessity and methods of effective public relations, advertising, and solicitation schemes. It could expose the practical workings of labor-management relations, feuds, and resolutions. It could trace the development and application of new technologies. Lastly, but not least, it could provide sociological insights into mercantile titans, calculating politicians, defensive labor leaders, and agitated community like attitude of maritime Massachusetts [supports the contention that] far better had the brains and energy that produced the clipper ships been put into the iron screw steamer."[23]

The Civil War contributed further to the crumbling of Boston's commercial prestige. The Port's large trade with the South was disrupted, export cotton for the European trade was cut off, and freight rates increased due to Confederate raiders. After the war, however, despite various trade fluctuations, Boston experienced a gradual and general commercial advance between 1865 and 1900. It was the railroad that temporarily rescued Boston.

The complexion of Boston's foreign trade did not change greatly except for an increasing emphasis on imported goods and raw materials. The transatlantic trade with England and Europe was still paramount as Boston continued to hold the dominant position in dealings with the Mediterranean. Though New York supplanted Boston as the terminus of the Far East trade, and commerce with India and Africa decreased after 1860, these losses were compensated for by expanding trade with South America and a new trade with Australia. The goods carried back to New England on these routes were the familiar industrial necessities; hides and skins for tanneries and shoe factories; cotton and wool for textile mills; jute for bagging factories; hemp for linen thread mills; sisal for cordage works; sugar for refineries; and chemicals, drugs, and dyes for chemical and fertilizer works.

It was the domestic trade, however, on which the Port relied for the bulk of its total tonnage. The growth of domestic imports continued to reflect the steady industrial expansion of New England. This growth was more marked than that of any of Boston's leading outport competitors. From Maine to the Gulf of Mexico flowed the goods so imperative for the region's industrial economy. Principal inbound cargoes included sugar, molasses, sand, lumber, and vast amounts of coal, raw cotton, and domestic wool. Coal was the most important tonnage commodity in this coastal trade, and the Chesapeake Bay offered an endless supply for the furnaces of northern factories.

The key to Boston's success during this period, however, was the great volume of exports the Port was able to muster to counterbalance the huge volume of imported fuel and raw materials. By the end of the century, in fact, Boston experienced an unusual excess of outbound over inbound cargoes. This resulted primarily from two developments. First was the rise of the great New England textile centers after 1880, which catapulted Boston into the position of a world wool market second only to London. Even this, however, while demanding additional imports of raw materials, did not give Boston a sufficient export base. Increased textiles supplemented the Port's other exports, and outgoing cargoes of manufactured goods increased. These increases, although adding value to Boston's export traffic, did not supply the much needed bulk to fill ships. The Port's dilemma of high-value–low-bulk exports was exacerbated by the fact that most of the area's manufactured products continued to be absorbed domestically. This same condition plagues Boston today.

The bulk exports Boston could not find in its immediate hinterland it discovered in the fecund farms of the Midwest. The trunk lines of the great American railroads were built to transport western produce, especially grain, not to the relatively sparsely populated East, but rather to voracious Europe. All the major North Atlantic Ports came to rely on carloads of Midwestern grain for needed bulk exports. Only New York, almost embarrassed by the amount of varied freight seeking its port, escaped this singular dependence. However, Boston, Philadelphia, and Baltimore fought among themselves for grain shipments from the great American interior. The situation illustrated a basic axiom: "A port is not the origin or destination of the bulk of traffic carried by its water lines. It is a concentration point or gateway, in severe competition with other gateways for the business of a common hinterland."[24] In this particular competition, the North Atlantic ports were the combatants, railroads were the weapons, and Midwest grain was the prize.

Boston interests took the initiative in exploiting the unprecedented opportunity offered by a western rail connection. In 1842, they pushed through a line to Albany, which already had connections with Buffalo, and Boston was the first port to establish an all-rail route to tap western export potential. This burst of entrepreneurial energy was made possible by the fact that Boston's general business health was least affected among eastern commercial centers by the Panic of 1837 and the subsequent depression. Added to the early benefits of Cunard's exclusive serivce, this combination of advantages swung the tide of battle in Boston's direction and the Port regained a position of leadership in the North Atlantic rivalry for the first time in many years. Moreover, it equipped Boston to present a genuine threat to New York, as the railroad's capacity for uninterrupted service soon demonstrated its inherent superiority over any inland waterway susceptible to winter freeze-overs. This understandably shook New York's complacency about its invincible Erie Canal. Along with sole access to Cunard's steamships, however, this fortunate circumstance was shortlived. By 1852, New York, Philadelphia, and Baltimore had responded to the challenge and established their own rail lines to the west. As expected, it was not long before New York emerged on top on the merits of its singularly entrenched concentration of trade.

Once the rail boom was underway, the major railroads expended great efforts to build up their respective ports. Norfolk was served by the Norfolk & Western and Newport News by the Chesapeake & Ohio. Baltimore was the home port of the Baltimore & Ohio, but was also served by the Pennsylvania and the Western Maryland. Philadelphia had the Pennsylvania as well as the Baltimore & Ohio and the Reading. New York, in a class by itself, was served by all the home roads of its competitors plus three direct routes of its own to Chicago — the Erie, and two lines of the New York Central — and had two additional strong roads to Buffalo — the Delaware, Lackawanna & Western and the Lehigh Valley. Boston was served by the Boston & Maine, the Boston & Albany, and the New York, New Haven & Hartford.

# Foreword

The purpose of the Lexington Books Series on Marine Affairs is to bring significant contributions in marine affairs and policy to the marine community. The series consists of monographs on important contemporary problems; and combines high quality with the fast production which is so essential in such a rapidly changing field.

Louis Cellineri's *Seaport Dynamics* makes a significant contribution to the series. He has addressed an important problem, that is, how does one evaluate a major port facility so that it can be economically viable, and flexible enough to accommodate changing needs? Although the major focus of the work is on the port of Boston, the lessons and analyses clearly have much wider applicability.

As Cellineri remarks in quoting Alfred E. Smith, "Outside of the Eighteenth Amendment, port development is about as dry a subject as you can think of." This is definitely not the case with this book. Cellineri handles the complex subject in an interesting way so that it should be of interest to students of history, political science, and marine affairs.

John King Gamble, Jr.
December 5, 1975

# List of Tables

# Contents

**Seaport Dynamics**

factions. The Port of Boston could educationally provide encouraging and discouraging illustrations in all of these fields.

Ports — as their handmaidens, ships — often assume characters of their own and become almost humanized participants in their own chronicles. The Port of Boston has enjoyed and suffered most of the vicissitudes offered by maritime commerce, from an internationally glorious significance to a nationally inglorious insignificance. It has been a versatile Thespian, dramatic and melodramatic, tragic and burlesque. Above all, it has faithfully served and reflected its assigned hinterland, from an initial national expanse to a contrained local market.

The seaport was the vital link in the early flow of European settlers, most of life's necessities, and all communication with the outside world; later, it was the gateway for the raw materials of rapid and extensive industrialization. Now, its most visible purpose is to serve as the terminus of a troublesome energy lifeline. It once accommodated an endless variety of offerings and demands, and, now, with singular dependence, receives one predominant import and is only beginning to recapture significant exports. It has attracted and lost those waterfront industries that impart so much to the dynamism of a past Boston or a present Rotterdam. It once supported a thriving and integrated maritime economic structure only to witness its gradual erosion and the alien expropriation of its ownership and control. From a premier distribution center that generated revenues for all port interests, it has declined to a status at which its very economic viability has been questioned. This near dismissal in certain circles of the present and potential value of shipping in Boston only presents another dilemma to those attempting to cope with this veritable maritime can of worms.

But despite all these obstacles, the Port may possibly, for the first time in many years, face the opportunity of genuine resuscitation. In proper context, however, with so many variables, contingencies, and external influences, the only reasonable undertaking may be a brief survey of the Port's past, a description of its present, and a modest anticipation of its future. Too presumptuous a hindsight or a prescience would unjustly open the Pandora's box that the seaport's revivalists are endeavoring to seal. The purpose of this study is not to reach any final conclusions but rather to present the Port of Boston in a broad, balanced, and hopefully useful perspective. The end result is not as thorough and detailed as the Port deserves. Nevertheless, it may provide some helpful background for those who will directly or indirectly influence the future of the Port, and, more importantly, may contribute in a small way to focusing more public interest on a valuable but generally ignored public resource. If New York's Governor Smith could convince his audience of a port's inherent interest, maybe someday someone can convince a currently inattentive audience of the inherent worth of the Port of Boston.

Table 1-2
**Exports and Imports of Principal North Atlantic Ports, 1821–1860**
(based on totals for respective states)

*(millions of dollars)*

| | Total U.S. | | New York | | Boston | | Philadelphia | | Baltimore | |
|---|---|---|---|---|---|---|---|---|---|---|
| | Exports | Imports | Exports | Imports | Exports | Imports | Exports | Imports | Exports | Imports |
| 1821 | 64 | 62 | 13 | 23 | 12 | 14 | 7 | 8 | 3 | 4 |
| 1830 | 73 | 70 | 19 | 35 | 7 | 10 | 4 | 8 | 3 | 4 |
| 1840 | 132 | 107 | 34 | 60 | 10 | 16 | 6 | 8 | 5 | 4 |
| 1850 | 151 | 178 | 52 | 111 | 10 | 30 | 4 | 12 | 6 | 6 |
| 1860 | 400 | 362 | 145 | 248 | 17 | 41 | 5 | 14 | 9 | 9 |

*Source:* R.G. Albion with Jennie Barnes Pope, *The Rise of the Port of New York, 1915–1860* (New York: Charles Scribners' Sons 1939), appendix II and III, pp. 390, 391. Copyright 1939 Charles Scribners' Sons. (Figures compiled from annual Reports on Commerce and Navigation.)

world trade center and the profits of a great distribution center. Boston's outbound cargoes remained stationary for the lack of a good export base, and even its imports grew more slowly than New York's. (See Table 1-2.) Boston could still outpace Philadelphia and Baltimore because local ownership of a large share of the American merchant fleet guaranteed it cargoes. Competition with New York, however, was a losing battle. Boston was critically handicapped by its primary reliance on local enterprise for its sustenance and struggled with the persistent and more and more apparent dilemma of an increasingly imbalanced trade, which eventually relegated it to the status of a second-rate outport.

Boston's situation was hurt rather than helped by its response to steam power. Though it scored an impressive headstart over its rival ports, Boston's overall adaptation to this revolutionary technology was disastrously inept. In 1840, through offers of free facilities, the Port induced Samuel Cunard to use Boston as the U.S. terminus via Halifax of his North American Royal Mail Steam Packet Company, which was subsidized by the British government. For eight years, Boston reaped the exclusive and considerable advantages of this regular service and maintained a decided edge over its competitors. Local efforts to establish Boston-based lines, however, were neither aggressive nor successful. The record was one of costly failures in transatlantic ventures and only a very slow establishment of coastwise steam packet service. Up to the Civil War, Boston played a practically negligible role in the development of American steamship lines.

New York, in contrast, got off to a weak start but soon became the focus of steam activity in the United States. Though hampered by Cunard's initial decision, New York interests were able to capture most subsequent U.S. government mail subsidies. This opportunity for regular steamliner service was frustrated, however, by inneffective operations — such as the fast but unprofitable Collins Steamship Line to England — and the government ended all subsidies in 1850. New York's real benefactors proved to be foreign rather than domestic. In 1848, Cunard began a better and direct service between Liverpool and New York, bowing to the fact that cargoes habitually using New York could not be diverted to Boston. The same pattern attracted other British and German lines — the real pioneers of steam transport — and soon New York overshadowed Boston.

Sailing ships had so well secured New York's supremacy that steamships were bound to accomodate themselves to it. The steampship also bolstered New York's postwar position as the shipbuilding center of the United States before the Civil War, with the great East River yards turning out the highest quality sail and steam ocean vessels. Boston, of course, suffered in the process. Equally damaging was Boston's loss of traditional traffic when New York inaugurated steamship service to the deep South in the 1830s and 1840s. Boston's inability to exploit this new technology drove local talent and capital to New York to seek better opportunities and more assured investments. Hindsight on this "ostrich-

All these roads attempted to establish European steamship lines, thus being able to haul import and export traffic for the interior. In some cases, if independent carriers could not be convinced to enter its port, a railroad would establish its own steamship services. More often, however, a steamship line was attracted on the understanding that railroad and steamship lines would work together for their mutual interests and by the offer of a free pier, a practice to which only New York did not need to resort. This was the general method used in Boston. The Port's railroads were able to entice steamship lines with offers of free piers, guaranteed cargoes, and new terminal facilities such as warehouses and grain elevators. Only the railroads could afford this sales program, for only they received the lucrative compensation of the rail haul freights which the steamship lines generated; moreover the rail lines enjoyed the equally important advantages resulting from controlling the volume and timing of supply.

So it was western grain, produce, and livestock, supplemented by local manufactured goods, that dramatically increased Boston's export trade. Though the steamship had a late start in Boston, by 1880, 322 steamers carried merchandise to European ports, and, in 1900, only 2,686 of the 10,436 ships entering Boston depended on sails.[25] By 1900, Boston was still the nation's second largest port in foreign trade with $192,609,000 of overseas commerce, 50 percent more than its nearest rival, Baltimore. Surpassed only by New York with $1,068,700,000, Boston handled approximately one-fifth of the country's aggregate foreign tonnage.[26] The Port's status, however, was shaky and its vulnerable commerical trade base proved unreliable.

Beginning about 1900, Boston suffered a serious dislocation of its trade that was ultimately to result in irreversible deterioration. By 1920, the earlier predictions of the Port's fall from glory were realized; Boston faced a dismal future. The artificial stimulation of World War I brought unparalleled activity to the Port of Boston. Unprecedented exports of meat, dairy products, breadstuffs, cotton, leather, iron, steel, and munitions were shipped to Europe. This was, however, a fleeting respite from a persistent pattern that eroded Boston's stature in world commerce.

Although the value of Boston's foreign commerce increased impressively between 1900 and 1920, it did not match the gains of the other U.S. North Atlantic ports and marked a preponderance of imports over exports that was destined to be magnified. (See Table 1-3.) Boston's overall tonnage gain compared favorably with that of its rival ports, but these total figures were deceptive. (See Table 1-4.) The Port's coastal trade, which became the dominant activity in its commercial traffic, labored under a more severe imbalance than its foreign trade. (See Table 1-5.)

The stimulus behind Boston's increased seaborne traffic during this period was, predictably, the development of new and expanded manufacturing industries and their unquenchable thirst for raw materials. (See Table 1-6.) The Port continued to receive many of these necessities from foreign trade. Vast quantities of grain materials from the East Indies, Australia, Egypt, Argentina, and

**Table 1–3**
**Foreign Imports and Exports, 1919, 1929**

(short tons)

| | 1919 | | 1929 | |
|---|---|---|---|---|
| | *Imports* | *Exports* | *Imports* | *Exports* |
| Total U.S. | 19,882,693 | 48,240,771 | 57,975,796 | 69,534,481 |
| Atlantic Coastal Ports | 13,167,893 | 30,101,459 | 40,401,769 | 19,372,216 |
| Boston | 1,465,251 | 1,366,708 | 3,261,301 | 303,120 |

*Source:* U.S. Army, *Report of the Chief of Engineers, 1920,* (Washington, D.C.: U.S. Government Printing Office, 1921), part 3.

U.S. Army Corps of Engineers, *Waterborne Commerce of the United States, Calendar Year 1929,* (Washington, D.C.: U.S. Government Printing Office, 1930), parts 2 and 5.

more than forty other countries were included among the Port's inbound cargoes. It remained the second largest foreign import center behind New York and the leading wool market in the United States. By 1929, Boston's foreign import tonnage had risen to a record 3,261,301 tons.[27]

It was Boston's domestic trade, however, that occupied an increasing proportion of its maritime activities. (See Table 1-7.) Throughout the early twentieth century, Boston's coastal trade ranked second only to New York and through the 1920s constituted over two-thirds of the Port's entire business. Unfortunately, coastal receipts greatly outnumbered coastal shipments with vast and growing amounts of raw materials arriving from the Gulf of Mexico, other North Atlantic ports, and later even the West Coast. With no indigenous natural resources of its own, New England was still forced to rely on imports to feed its population and sustain its industrial growth. Coal became the leading import product, doubling to 3,000,000 tons from 1902 to 1916 and comprising over 60 percent of the coastal receipts through the 1920s. The character of Boston's foreign and domestic imports is reflected in Table 1-8.

It was Boston's reduced export base that dealt the death blow. While New England tool and machinery production had developed extensively, it presented the familiar dilemma of high-value–low-bulk goods unable to fill departing ships and, in any case, primarily absorbed domestically. More critical to Boston's commercial traffic was the loss of Midwest grain, upon which the Port had become dependent for bulk exports. The net result of this situation was a rapid decline in foreign-export trade. The Port's share of total national foreign exports dropped from 8.2 percent in 1882, to 2.3 percent in 1920, and to less than 1 percent in 1929. Boston was surpassed in foreign exports by Baltimore in 1905 and by Philadelphia in 1908. By 1929, with only 303,120 tons of overseas

Table 1–4
Waterborne Commerce of the U.S. and the North Atlantic Ports, 1919, 1929

(short tons)

| Year | Total U.S. | Boston | New York | Philadelphia | Baltimore | Hampton Roads |
|------|-----------|--------|----------|--------------|-----------|---------------|
| 1919 | 319,762,727 | 8,680,243 | 140,354,096 (estimate) | 23,895,976 | 14,055,906 | 21,618,071 |
| 1929 | 519,870,279 | 19,065,050 | 182,988,041 | 30,252,422 | 20,264,165 | 25,116,481 |

Source: U.S. Army, Report of the Chief of Engineers, 1920, (Washington, D.C.: U.S. Government Printing Office, 1921), part 3. U.S. Army Corps of Engineers, Waterborne Commerce of the United States, Calendar Year 1929, (Washington, D.C.: U.S. Government Printing Office, 1930), part 2.

Table 1-5
Waterborne Commerce Through the Port of Boston, 1905-1929

(short tons)

| | Foreign | | | |
|---|---|---|---|---|
| Year | Import | Export | Domestic | Total* |
| 1905 | 974,712 | 1,294,815 | 5,289,764 | 7,559,291 |
| 1910 | 765,500 | 1,256,892 | 5,304,453 | 7,326,845 |
| 1920 | 1,673,899 | 573,489 | 7,023,605 | 9,270,993 |
| 1925 | 2,586,065 | 338,779 | 11,187,691 | 14,112,535 |
| 1928 | 2,964,876 | 403,486 | 12,734,997 | 16,103,359 |
| 1929 | 3,261,301 | 303,120 | 14,444,765 | 19,065,050 |

*Total includes "other domestic."

Source: U.S. Army, Report of the Chief of Engineers, 1920, (Washington, D.C.: U.S. Government Printing Office, 1921), part 3.

U.S. Army Corps of Engineers, Waterborne Commerce of the United States, Calendar Year 1929 (Washington, D.C.: U.S. Government Printing Office, 1930), part 2.

Table 1-6
Industrial Growth of New England States, 1889, 1904, 1909

| Year | Number of plants | Capital employed | Workmen employed | Raw material used | Sale of product |
|---|---|---|---|---|---|
| 1909 | 23,351 | $2,503,854,000 | 1,101,290 | $1,476,297,000 | $2,670,650,000 |
| 1904 | 22,279 | 1,870,995,000 | 940,752 | 1,116,273,000 | 2,025,999,000 |
| 1899 | 22,576 | 1,507,630,000 | – | 994,037,000 | 1,660,348,000 |

Source: U.S. Department of Commerce, Bureau of the Census, Bulletin of the Census Bureau on Manufactures in the United States, 1910 (Washington, D.C.: U.S. Government Printing Office, 1911).

exports, Boston ranked eighteenth among all U.S. ports.[28] Domestic receipts of bulk imports continued to sustain the Port's activity; Boston's coastal arrivals soon exceeded those of both New York and Philadelphia.

Although imports were greater than exports along almost the entire North Atlantic seaboard, the disparity was greatest at Boston, where the ratio of imports to exports was 4 to 1 in 1920 and 10 to 1 in 1929. While this traffic allowed substantial growth in overall tonnage, it became increasingly damaging to Boston's actual commercial state.

A number of interrelated factors exposed the vulnerability of the Port of Boston and paved the way for an era of stagnation. One national trend during

**Table 1–7**

**Total Waterborne Commerce Through the Port of Boston, 1919, 1929**

**(short tons)**

| Year | Foreign | | Domestic | | | Total |
| | Imports | Exports | Coastwise recipts | Coastwise shipments | Other domestic | |
|------|---------|---------|-----------|-----------|-----------|-------|
| 1919 | 1,465,251 | 1,366,708 | 5,075,399 | 772,885 | – | 8,680,243 |
| 1929 | 3,261,301 | 303,120 | 12,742,708 | 1,712,057 | 1,045,864 | 19,065,050 |

*Source:* U.S. Army, *Report of the Chief of Engineers, 1920,* (Washington, D.C.: U.S. Government Printing Office, 1921), part 3.

U.S. Army Corps of Engineers, *Waterborne Commerce of the United States, Calendar Year 1929* (Washington, D.C.: U.S. Government Printing Office, 1930), part 2.

this period affected all North Atlantic ports. The United States began to consume the agricultural production upon which all these ports had previously relied for bulk exports. This led to increased competition for the remaining Midwest produce. Other developments, however, hurt Boston in particular. In the early twentieth century, Canada became increasingly sea-conscious and diverted much of its previous business through Boston to its own ports at St. John's and Halifax. Boston came to handle only the occasional overflow of farm produce from these ports. Furthermore, Boston's thriving export trade with Liverpool, the gateway to the North English industrial area – at the time the world's largest consumer of imported foodstuffs – effectively disappeared. Boston, with its northerly latitude and cool adjacent water, had always been favored for the export of livestock and provisions and, in the late nineteenth century, had led the country in the European cattle trade. However, dwindling farm exports and a growing British preference for Canadian and Argentine cattle reduced the Port's exports of cattle from 16,620 head in 1897 to practically none by 1929.[29] Lastly, in 1902, the International Mercantile Marine was formed, consolidating the major U.S. lines to the United Kingdom, and established its headquarters in New York. It absorbed the three major Boston-to-England lines – the Leyland Line, the Dominion Line, and the Wilson-Furness-Leyland Line – and the city lost its independent management of these services. Local management had tended to fill ships at any cost, but these lines would not get western exports if they did not come through Boston. Under the new consolidated control, cargoes would be available at New York, Philadelphia, or Baltimore; and Boston lost much of the frequency and regularity of its North Atlantic service. This hastened the attrition of Boston-owned vessels. By 1929, except for a few vessels in the Canada trade and some locally owned tankers and colliers, Boston did not have a single ship of its own engaged in foreign commerce. The once great shipowner-merchant community had been displaced by fleets under outside control, and

**Table 1-8**
**Leading Freight Through the Port of Boston, 1910, 1929**

(short tons)

| | Foreign | | | | | | Domestic | |
| --- | --- | --- | --- | --- | --- | --- | --- | --- |
| | Imports | | Exports | | Coastwise receipts | | Coastwise shipments* | |
| **1910** | Wood and wood manufactures | 299,923 | Breadstuffs | 267,563 | Coal | 7,151,629 | | |
| | Sugar | 204,482 | Iron and steel manufactures | 88,031 | Oil | 221,594 | | |
| | Fibres, grasses, and manufactures | 119,532 | Meat and dairy products | 77,745 | Sugar | 157,000 | | |
| | Fruits and nuts | 94,312 | Wood manufactures | 56,293 | Lumber | 64,711 | | |
| | Chemicals, drugs, and dyes | 67,004 | Hides and skins | 54,015 | Sand and gravel | 27,592 | Refined petroleum products | 371,676 |
| | | | Wool | 40,586 | | | Fuel oil | 365,327 |
| | | | Cotton | 29,535 | | | Pig iron | 85,864 |
| | | | | | | | Fertilizer | 40,900 |
| **1929** | Crude petroleum | 520,823 | Wheat | 56,563 | Coal | 6,905,464 | | |
| | Sugar | 431,884 | Wheat flour | 34,247 | Crude oil | 2,437,948 | | |
| | Fuel oil | 384,957 | Barley | 45,759 | Refined petroleum products | 641,528 | | |
| | Coal | 307,229 | Iron and steel scrap | 38,485 | Fuel oil | 577,413 | | |
| | Woodpulp and cellulose | 237,531 | Paper | 10,725 | Sand and gravel | 551,939 | | |
| | Ore | 152,089 | | | Lumber and logs | 379,302 | | |
| | Lumber | 103,582 | | | Fish | 127,861 | | |
| | | | | | Gasoline | 107,752 | | |
| | | | | | Wool | 35,526 | | |

*Source:* Report of the Chief Engineer, 1920, Part 3. Corps of Engineers, 1930, Part 2.
*Combined domestic commerce for 1910; not differentiated as coastwise receipts and shipments until 1929. Vast majority of this combined total, however, was made up of coastwise receipts.

the local employment, revenues, and preferential treatment generated by the earlier maritime structure were lost forever.

Though these events contributed to Boston's decline, the major villains in the Port's drama were the railroads, the heroes of an earlier age. Boston had been at a disadvantage since the development of the great American rail systems. For years, North Atlantic ports have been of two types, New York and all the others. Since the completion of the Erie Canal, western traffic had naturally sought New York. The railroads accommodated themselves to New York's preeminence and all trunk lines were concentrated at the port, perpetuating its monopoly of the western export trade. In the competition for a share of the total western volume of exports, Boston was distinctly handicapped among the North Atlantic outports. It was the only port without a line west of the Hudson River, and, hence, no western export traffic could be funneled directly to Boston. The Boston railroads were dependent upon the traffic handed over to them at switching points by carriers who were primarily interested in taking these exports to their home ports, giving them the longest hauls and the largest earnings. Not only did the Boston railroads have to absorb these switching charges, but the Port was forced to rely on the northern trunk lines located in New York which, in effect, controlled the local lines. Since the interests of these trunk lines always centered about another port, Boston got very little business directed to it from the interior hinterland.

The local structure and operations of Boston's railroads aggravated these disadvantages. The three Boston lines owned and maintained three separate piers. This diversified ownership of the waterfront resulted in utter confusion of wharfage and dockage rates which hampered traffic movement through the Port. More harmful, however, were the mutually exclusive relationships between the railroads and their respective steamship lines. Having supplied a steamship line with a free pier, a Boston rail carrier saw the line as an extension of the railroad and attempted to monopolize the traffic moving by means of that extension. It would be established under contract that the steamship line, wholly or to the greatest possible extent, would only do its export and import business with one particular railroad. Each steamship line became preferentially bound to a single rail carrier. Instead of having all Boston railroads working for every steamship line, each line was committed to a single road and no steamship line could berth at the terminal of more than one railroad. Competition for freight was thus stifled and operations became inflexible. This inflexibility was further sustained by a system of switching charges. If a railroad carried freight for a steamship line other than one of its own, it suffered a switching charge to move that freight over the pier of the railroad to which the line was contracted. This practice was common to all North Atlantic ports without a public belt line serving all terminals. New York, however, had the distinct advantage of an extensive and free lighterage system that could transport export freight from any railroad to any steamer in the harbor. Through these lighters, all piers could be easily reached by all railroads. This system's capacity, flexibility, convenience, and ease of expansion were far superior to any belt line.[30]

Although all of these elements contributed to Boston's decline, they were minor compared to the loss of western grain exports due to a discriminatory railroad rate differential. In the intense competition for Midwest exports, the major trunk lines had waged a series of disasterous rate wars. Several unsuccessful attempts were made to divide this traffic and establish compensatory rates for carrying it. Finally, the railroads reached an agreement on import-export commerce in 1877 that bore some relation to relative distance and cost of service. Philadelphia was allowed an export rate 2¢ per hundredweight (40¢ per ton) lower than New York, and Baltimore was allowed 3¢ lower (60¢ per ton) than New York. Boston was assigned the same rate as New York.[31]

In 1880, dissatisfied with this arrangement, New York withdrew from the agreement, and the worst rate war of all soon followed. In 1882, the dispute was submitted to a prestigious arbitration commission. The commission reaffirmed the 1877 agreement and further extended the preferential rates of Philadelphia and Baltimore to imports. This decision was accepted and, with minor modifications, remained the basis of the relative rate structure until 1963. The primary justification for these port differentials was the principle of competition. Because Boston was nearest to Europe and the channels of Philadelphia and Baltimore were not as deep as those of Boston and New York, these southern ports had traditionally had higher ocean rates to Great Britian and the Continent. Tramp steamers, handling most of the grain cargo at the time, charged Philadelphia and Baltimore rates 2¢ and 3¢ per hundredweight higher, respectively, than those at Boston and New York.[32] It was felt, therefore, that unless throughrates from the Midwest to England and Europe were equalized, no traffic would flow through the higher cost southern ports. By compensating for this with an exact counterbalance of inland rates, all North Atlantic ports were theoretically put on an equal footing to attract competitive freight.

At first, Boston did not feel the full effects of this preferential rate system. Export and import rates were not rigidly maintained and when the Boston roads needed western traffic for their steamship lines, they cut their rates and got the business. In 1903, however, the enactment of the Elkins Law, which required strict adherence to prescribed freight rates, put an end to this practice. From then on, Boston began to realize the full impact of port differentials (See Table 1-9.)

Exacerbating this situation was the increasing competition of New Orleans and Montreal for import freight. These two ports recognized that to attract regular steamer service to carry cotton from the Gulf and grain from Canada they had to generate imports for ships returning from Europe. To accomplish this, the railroads of both ports drastically reduced their import rail rates to levels equal to or lower than those of Baltimore. In 1909, another rate war ensued.

In 1911, it was decided to submit both import and export disputes to the Interstate Commerce Commission. In its decision the following year, the com-

**Table 1-9**
**Full Cargoes of Grain Shipped Through Specified Ports, 1908-1913**

|              | 1908 | 1909 | 1910 | 1911 | 1912 | 1913 |
|--------------|------|------|------|------|------|------|
| Baltimore    | 1    | 5    | 9    | 18   | 66   | 130  |
| Philadelphia | 19   | 12   | 1    | 16   | 34   | 34   |
| New York     | 0    | 5    | 0    | 4    | 26   | 45   |
| Boston       | 0    | 0    | 0    | 0    | 1    | 6    |

*Source:* Edwin J. Clapp, *The Port of Boston* (New Haven: Yale University Press, 1916), p. 120.

mission ordered the status quo maintained for all ports on both imports and exports. Boston's foreign commerce was now really threatened.

Four years later, the Port of Boston's fate was sealed. In 1916, the North Atlantic Conference of steamship lines operating in the overseas trade equalized ocean rates to all North Atlantic ports. This decision deprived Boston of its only competitive advantage in relation to through inland-ocean rates, namely, the lower ocean tariffs that naturally accrued to the U.S. North Atlantic port closest to Europe. Boston still remained 194 miles closer to Liverpool than New York, 337 miles closer than Philadelphia, and 493 miles closer than Baltimore, but these geographic actualities would no longer be relevant.

These developments forced upon Boston a crippling handicap in the intense competition among Atlantic ports for the critical traffic of the western hinterland. Import rates to the designated Central Freight Association Territory were lower via St. John's, Halifax, Montreal, Portland, Philadelphia, Baltimore, and Norfolk. More importantly, export rates from the west were lower via Montreal, Philadelphia, Baltimore, and Norfolk. Boston's dependence on this area was such that, in 1911, nearly 78 percent of the Port's export tonnage originated outside New England. (See Table 1-10.) This "unique form of torture," as ex-Governor Thomas E. Dewey described it to the Supreme Court, was to persist for over fifty years despite constant legal efforts by both New York and Boston.

While Boston's rival North Atlantic outports were formally granted this decided advantage, Boston was theoretically allotted equality with New York. This parity, based on a myopic consideration of only equal rail rates, was illusory. New York enjoyed advantages and afforded inducements that attracted a large portion of the interior commerce that might otherwise have gone through Boston. The New York State Barge Canal System gave the city the most extensive arrangement of inland waterways. Its harbor was connected to Lake Erie, Lake Ontario, and Lake Champlain by all-water routes. By 1937, over 5 million tons of cargo were carried over these waterways. The historical concentration of western traffic in the largest port continued, further enhanced by expanding facilities and a superlative lighterage system. With the great number of ships calling on New York, opportunities absent in Boston could be offered to shippers of grain. A parcel of grain sent to New York for shipment several weeks ahead of time would have a chance to get "distress room" on another steamer sailing immediately. This "distress room" diversion meant a lower freight rate to the shipper because the departing ship, unable to acquire a full cargo, would carry the grain for next to nothing rather than sail half empty. Storing grain in New York while awaiting sale for export was also more advantageous. Such grain had a choice of shipment on any of New York's numerous steamship lines. At Boston, on the other hand, with its limited steamship services and its inflexible terminal arrangement, transshipment of stored grain was usually restricted to only those few lines that were allied with the particular rail carrier that had made the inland delivery.

**Table 1-10**
**Percentage Division of Export Tonnage via Boston,**
**Year Ending June 30, 1911**

|  | From New England | From U.S. points other than New England | | |
|---|---|---|---|---|
|  | Percent | Grain | Other traffic | Total |
| Boston & Albany | 15.1 | 44.6% | 40.3% | 100% |
| Boston & Maine | 26.4 | 25.5 | 48.1 | 100 |
| Average | 22.1 | 32.7 | 45.2 | 100 |

Source: Edwin J. Clapp, *The Port of Boston* (New Haven: Yale University Press, 1916).

More determinant, however, was New York's ability to absorb charges for accessory services, which Boston and other outports had to assess the shipper or consignee. Since the city owned all covered piers, New York did not levy wharfage charges for merchandise using such a pier. "Side-wharfage" for handling goods between ship and lighter was also free, as was the entire lighterage system. The New York railroads, moreover, offered free grain elevators and low warehouse rates. In Boston, with its dispersed and privately owned waterfront, the three local railroads charged for all these services. Along with the switching charges cited earlier, this high-cost structure for shipments through Boston gave New York an even greater competitive advantage.

Port interests perceived that Boston was further impeded in the contest for freight traffic by the absence of independent control over its carriers. As noted earlier, the Port's three railroads were at the mercy of trunk lines whose primary allegiance was to rival ports and its major steamship lines had fallen under New York control. Boston's traditionally defensive attitude toward New York aroused suspicions that the local rail lines were being manipulated to the benefit of other ports and to the detriment of Boston. Eventually, the Port's three rail carriers came gradually "under the domination if not actual control of foreign railroads."[33] The Pennsylvania Railroad owned controlling stock in the Boston & Maine and the New York, New Haven & Hartford. Boston's distrust, however, was vented most toward New York. The leasing of the Boston & Albany to the New York Central aroused the conviction that the local line was not allowed by its mother line to grant the valuable inducements of free services to attract traffic that was the practice of all New York rail carriers. The Boston shipping community felt that such policies were deliberately followed to minimize competition from the Port and assure its status as a secondary transportation unit.

All of these developments severing Boston from the common Midwest hinterland, had dire consequences for the Port's maritime commerce. Since the majority of imports destined for the Midwest at the time were coarse commodities — such as, clay, fish, ores, brewers rice, and burlap — their transport was influenced by slight differences in through rates. Ocean rates being equal, Boston's outport competitors could attract most of this traffic because their lower rail import rates gave them a lower through rate from foreign ports to the American interior. This lack of western imports, however, was primarily a railroad problem. Boston had never had such trouble since great amounts of imports were readily absorbed by New England itself. The railroads, without sufficient imports, were forced to send back west empty box cars that had brought food and raw materials east.

Unfortunately, the loss of Midwest exports was more severely damaging for Boston. The Port's total foreign exports of grains dropped from 267,563 tons in 1910 to 136,783 tons in 1929 and to 7,863 tons by 1938.[34] The rate differential made it impossible to load the tramp steamers, which carried bulk inbound cargo to the Port, with outbound grain. Since they had to make an extra move to another port for export cargo, charter rates for imports to Boston were set higher than those to Philadelphia or Baltimore. New England manufacturers, reliant upon imported raw materials, were burdened with this additional expense.

The effect of the differential on liners using Boston was even more serious. The large and constant traffic between U.S. North Atlantic ports and Europe resulted in regular liner schedules with lower ocean rates than tramps. Such liner service is crucial for any port. The essence of a great seaport was aptly stated fifty years ago as

... the number and frequency of its water connection, particularly its over-seas lines. The traffic that feeds these lines consists of exports and imports for an extensive hinterland; the port is merely a gate through which this traffic passes.[35]

The same holds true today. Boston, then as now, was a rusty gate, unappealing to most cargo traffic.

The regular steamship lines out of Boston were forced to quote lower ocean rates for western cargo in order to compete with Philadelphia and Baltimore which had lower through rates based on lower rail rates. The differential led steamship companies to load export cargo at ports other than Boston. The loss of western grain and Boston's comparatively small amount of foreign shipments unbalanced the Port's foreign trade even further. (See Table 1-11.) A debilitating shipping pattern with Boston as the first port of call was established and continues to the present. With its great demand for imports, Boston became the first port a ship would visit to unload much of its cargo. Without sufficient outbound cargo available in Boston, the ship would proceed to New York and then to one or several of the other North Atlantic outports to unload its remaining cargo and take on exports. Finally, it would return to New York to complete its export cargo before sailing.

This pattern made Boston a favorable inbound port but a horrid outbound port. Once this indirect export service from Boston was established, it diverted shipments that would have naturally used the Port. The prime reason was the long delay when a ship left Boston, called on New York and another port or two, and eventually sailed for Europe. Gradually, this unfavorable export service was extended to include not just European ports, but most other world ports likely to receive shipments from Boston.

This situation was made even worse by a vicious cycle which resulted in a mass defection of local shippers to New York. Attracted by the frequency, multiplicity, and directness of the major port's steamship services, increasingly larger amounts of New England commodities were exported through New York. By the 1920s, about 65 percent (by value) of New England manufactures intended for export moved through New York, while only about 14 percent moved through Boston. This process was self-perpetuating; as Boston generated fewer outbound shipments, the frequency and regularity of liner service was further reduced. This in turn caused more local exports to sail from New York, further diminishing Boston's ability to supply overseas shipments; and so it went. This procedure continues today, despite the higher cost of transporting New England export products to New York by rail or truck.

So the once great Port of Boston was reduced to the humiliation of being a port of call rather than a major terminus of world trade. Natural conditions no longer governed the volume of traffic that might be expected geographically to flow through the Port. This new orientation was summarized with foresight when the downward spiral was just becoming obvious:

The determining factor is not nearness to European ports, but inland rates, speed and frequency of railroad service from the interior to the seaboard, inter-railroad alliances and feuds, the relative strength and zeal of soliciting forces in the interior, deep-rooted prejudices on the part of shippers, rates of ocean carriers, relative frequency of ocean service, coastwise services feeding ocean lines, and other

**Table 1-11**
**Boston Freight Traffic, 1929 (short tons)**

| Classes of commodities | Foreign | | Domestic, coastwise | | | Total |
|---|---|---|---|---|---|---|
| | Imports | Exports | Receipts | Shipments | Local | |
| Animals and animal products | 96,696 | 16,939 | 116,435 | 35,179 | 36 | 315,285 |
| Vegetable food products | 743,578 | 151,585 | 76,575 | 29,229 | 11,535 | 1,012,502 |
| Other vegetable products | 35,726 | 3,465 | 42,052 | 12,623 | – | 93,866 |
| Textiles | 253,676 | 18,388 | 131,055 | 55,189 | – | 458,308 |
| Wood and paper | 414,578 | 22,099 | 422,671 | 40,566 | 38,733 | 938,647 |
| Nonmetallic minerals | 1,449,746 | 3,714 | 11,301,764 | 913,953 | 549,510 | 14,218,687 |
| Ores, metals, manufactures of | 200,821 | 50,659 | 8,453 | 106,540 | 688 | 367,141 |
| Machinery | 5,676 | 4,693 | 4,207 | 3,682 | 60 | 18,318 |
| Chemicals | 33,578 | 28,273 | 131,194 | 78,326 | 8,783 | 280,154 |
| Unclassified | 27,226 | 3,305 | 458,302 | 436,770 | 436,539 | 1,362,142 |
| Total | 3,261,301 | 303,120 | 12,742,708 | 1,712,057 | 1,045,864 | 19,065,050 |

*Source*: U.S. Army Corps of Engineers, *Waterborne Commerce of the United States, Calendar Year 1929* (Washington, D.C.: U.S. Government Printing Office, 1930), part 2.

such factors. . . . Certain charges and practices at the seaboard, on the part of rail carriers, have an influence on traffic moving via the port they serve. Such matters are more intangible than geographical location and be beneath the surface of things.[36]

By 1920, these diverse factors had established the pattern that was to dominate Boston's future development. It seemed that all the historical flaws of Boston's maritime commerce converged, with a little assistance from the Interstate Commerce Commission, to seal the Port's fate. This period marked a watershed in Boston's history, just as the passing of the clipper ships had ended Massachusetts' independent maritime development. Only then, the transition brought Boston into the mainstream of America's commercial growth. Now, it segregated Boston as a languid Port with insignificant foreign trade and a consumptive reliance on imported bulk materials for its survivial. It regained a distinctive character, but this time it was the distinction of exclusion from the general trend of expansion of United States waterborne commerce.

Though total tonnage increased impressively to a record 19,065,050 tons in 1929, it masked the unhealthy nature of the Port's business. This growth was due solely to increased imports of raw materials, especially coastal receipts of coal. With the loss of western grain and the mounting desertion of New England shippers to New York, Boston's foreign trade deteriorated. The ruinous texture of the Port's commercial condition is reflected in Table 1-11.

After 1929, U.S. total tonnage grew and maintained an acceptable balance of trade by world shipping standards. However, Boston's total tonnage remained static, consistently hovering around 20 million tons. Until very recently, it experienced only minor fluctuations and the temporary disruptions of the Depression and World War II. (See Table 1-12).

Boston's competitive position has been further weakened by labor problems, deteriorating facilities, a rising cost structure, and community lethargy. Burdened with this reputation, it has lost ground to its competitors. All other North Atlantic ports have shared in the national progress, although their combined percentage share of total U.S. tonnage has been declining. Though they have experienced trade imbalances of about 3 to 1, these are not nearly so acute as Boston's 10 to 1 disequilibrium. The Port has made substantial gains in tonnage only recently, but still suffers its abnormally large excess of imports over exports.

Boston's status vis-à-vis the other North Atlantic ports is seen in Table 1-13. These comparisons are valid indicators of the Port's perennial troubles: a reliance on imported raw materials, especially domestic receipts and an insufficient base for either bulk or general cargo exports.

The character of Boston's commodity trade has changed little. (See Table 1-14.) Petroleum has displaced coal as the predominant import, in latter years amounting to 85 percent of the Port's total traffic. Scrap iron and tallow have

**Table 1-12**
**Net Waterborne Commerce Through the U.S.**
**and the Port of Boston, 1919–1972**
**(short tons)**

| Year | Net total waterborne commerce of the U.S. | Net total waterborne commerce of the port of Boston |
|------|------|------|
| 1919 | 319,762,727 | 8,680,243 |
| 1929 | 519,870,000 | 19,065,050 |
| 1932 | 286,494,000 | 14,012,172 |
| 1939 | 526,684,000 | 17,842,212 |
| 1941 | 623,837,000 | 18,826,770 |
| 1943 | 546,719,000 | 8,471,046 |
| 1945 | 605,594,000 | 12,850,522 |
| 1947 | 766,816,730 | 18,502,902 |
| 1950 | 820,583,571 | 19,446,897 |
| 1951 | 924,128,411 | 19,804,814 |
| 1952 | 887,721,984 | 19,961,128 |
| 1953 | 923,547,693 | 18,076,260 |
| 1954 | 867,640,207 | 17,878,336 |
| 1955 | 1,016,135,785 | 19,051,715 |
| 1956 | 1,092,912,924 | 20,977,834 |
| 1957 | 1,131,401,434 | 20,326,258 |
| 1958 | 1,004,515,776 | 19,275,022 |
| 1959 | 1,052,402,102 | 20,464,817 |
| 1960 | 1,099,850,431 | 19,019,567 |
| 1961 | 1,062,155,182 | 19,505,936 |
| 1962 | 1,129,404,375 | 18,984,380 |
| 1963 | 1,173,766,964 | 19,792,076 |
| 1964 | 1,238,093,573 | 20,011,441 |
| 1965 | 1,272,896,243 | 19,854,685 |
| 1966 | 1,334,116,078 | 20,287,217 |
| 1967 | 1,336,606,078 | 21,549,086 |
| 1968 | 1,395,839,450 | 22,610,760 |
| 1969 | 1,448,711,541 | 24,818,746 |
| 1970 | 1,531,696,507 | 26,867,918 |
| 1971 | 1,512,583,690 | 26,156,517 |
| 1972 | 1,616,792,605 | 26,483,438 |

*Source:* U.S. Army, *Report of the Chief of Engineers, 1920,* (Washington, D.C.: U.S. Government Printing Office, 1921), part 3. U.S. Army Corps of Engineers, *Waterborne Commerce of the United States, Calendar Years 1930–1972* (Washington, D.C.: U.S. Government Printing Office, 1931–1973), parts 1, 2 and 5.

demeaningly replaced once prestigious grain as the major bulk exports. In 1972, of 757,707 tons of foreign exports, scrap iron and steel accounted for 603,372 tons and tallow for 63,959 tons.[37] Moreover, all this type of import and export freight is handled over private facilities and generates minimal port revenues. Foreign commerce has also remained depressingly familiar. General cargo imports, principally food products, have come to constitute about 85 percent of the Port's total general cargo trade. New England manufactures continue to deprive Boston of an adequate overseas export medium.

**Table 1–13**
**Total Commerce Through Major North Atlantic**
**Ports, 1938, 1948, 1959, 1972 (short tons)**

| Port | Foreign | | Domestic | | |
| --- | --- | --- | --- | --- | --- |
| | Imports | Exports | Coastwise receipts | Coastwise shipments | Total * |
| *1938* | | | | | |
| Boston | 1,798,064 | 321,445 | 11,594,091 | 998,674 | 15,881,487 |
| New York | 11,063,421 | 6,663,303 | 30,911,353 | 7,074,593 | 147,655,675 |
| Philadelphia | 3,879,817 | 1,208,922 | 16,471,433 | 4,598,977 | 32,265,869 |
| Baltimore | 4,821,509 | 1,310,537 | 4,959,186 | 1,712,318 | 20,451,730 |
| Hampton Roads | 826,739 | 1,992,564 | 2,332,159 | 15,888,456 | 24,083,019 |
| *1948* | | | | | |
| Boston | 2,833,989 | 319,772 | 12,691,170 | 810,407 | 18,317,356 |
| New York | 19,678,027 | 10,259,918 | 42,364,833 | 8,952,384 | 180,884,287 |
| Philadelphia | 12,712,376 | 3,863,839 | 21,389,260 | 3,370,121 | 69,471,635 |
| Baltimore | 10,325,399 | 6,269,976 | 6,581,868 | 1,009,617 | 35,038,546 |
| Hampton Roads | 2,144,251 | 14,360,954 | 4,405,620 | 17,067,510 | 40,915,938 |
| *1959* | | | | | |
| Boston | 5,975,048 | 752,234 | 11,341,538 | 1,179,136 | 20,464,817 |
| New York | 39,108,306 | 6,808,863 | 43,643,002 | 13,582,417 | 154,155,873 |
| Philadelphia | 40,222,850 | 2,098,483 | 23,457,182 | 6,598,147 | 72,376,662 |
| Baltimore | 18,985,569 | 4,216,912 | 7,062,026 | 1,499,726 | 40,223,607 |
| Hampton Roads | 4,600,379 | 25,172,376 | 5,795,782 | 6,185,794 | 48,817,998 |
| *1972* | | | | | |
| Boston | 7,872,977 | 757,707 | 14,597,257 | 1,775,863 | 26,483,438 |
| New York | 10,243,429 | 13,537,963 | 20,106,413 | 9,467,539 | 117,865,396 |
| Philadelphia | 21,813,714 | 2,933,411 | 6,517,654 | 2,336,433 | 48,356,885 |
| Baltimore | 18,442,952 | 8,177,096 | 6,063,983 | 1,614,256 | 45,798,776 |
| Hampton Roads | 8,743,743 | 35,647,419 | 2,481,445 | 169,154 | 58,356,932 |

*Total includes "Internal Receipts and Shipments" and "Local."

Source: U.S. Army Corps of Engineers, *Waterborne Commerce of the United States, Calendar Years 1938, 1948, 1959, 1972* (Washington, D.C.: U.S. Government Printing Office, 1939, 1949, 1960, 1973), part 1.

The Port's suspended condition has felt the winds of change just recently. Whether, as with wars and depressions, this is only a temporary deviation from its deep-rooted, spiritless doldrums is uncertain. Boston as a seaport has, however, a heritage as glorious as its later repute has been inglorious. Its present dilemma is obviously not a novelty in historical perspective. But the Port's history certainly offers it numerous instances of stubborn Yankee determination and proud eras of commercial supremacy that it could more profitably emulate rather than resign itself to the more recent syndrome of frustration and stagnation.

Table 1-14
**Leading Freight Through the Port of Boston, 1972 (short tons)**

| Foreign | | | | Coastwise | | | |
|---|---|---|---|---|---|---|---|
| *Imports* | | *Exports* | | *Receipts* | | *Shipments* | |
| Crude petroleum | 128,195 | Tallow, animal fats, and oils | 63,959 | Gasoline | 5,048,306 | Gasoline | 286,162 |
| Limestone | 152,616 | Iron and steel scrap | 603,372 | Jet fuel | 610,549 | Kerosene | 134,485 |
| Salt | 212,951 | | | Kerosene | 125,777 | Distillate fuel oil | 982,282 |
| Sugar | 487,691 | | | Distillate fuel oil | 6,429,000 | Residual fuel oil | 204,612 |
| Lumber | 88,392 | | | Residual fuel oil | 1,504,674 | | |
| Gasoline | 91,724 | | | | | | |
| Kerosene | 372,204 | | | | | | |
| Residual fuel oil | 5,539,538 | | | | | | |
| Liquified gases | 89,881 | | | | | | |
| Coke, pet asphalts, and solvents | 105,685 | | | | | | |

*Source:* U.S. Army Corps of Engineers, *Waterborne Commerce of the United States, Calendar Year 1972* (Washington, D.C.: U.S. Government Printing Office, 1973), part 1.

# 2 Administration of the Port

*All authority is quite degrading.*
Oscar Wilde

From the mid-nineteenth century on, various administrative structures were established to arrest the decline and foster the development of the Boston seaport. The organization of these agencies varied, as did the administrative power and financial base that provided them. Eventually, the continual stagnation of Boston's maritime commerce and the ineffectiveness of these administrative experiments resulted in the creation of a modern, independent, and powerful Port Authority to guide the fortunes of the seaport.

Under Chapter 149 of the Acts of 1866, Massachusetts' first Board of Harbor Commissioners was established. It consisted of five unsalaried and part-time persons appointed by the governor for five-year terms. They were reimbursed expenses up to five dollars a day, for actual work done. They were entrusted with the care and supervision of all harbors in order to maintain unobstructed navigation and protect and develop the rights and property of the state. All work to be done in these harbors—such as the construction of bridges, wharves, and dams—required the approval of the board. The board was given some responsibility for preparing improvement plans but was only allowed appropriations expressly made by the legislature.

In 1877, the board was reestablished, along with a new Board of Land Commissioners.[1] The board retained its former power and duties, but was reduced to three persons appointed by the governor for three-year terms. In 1879, both of these boards were combined into the Board of Harbor and Land Commissioners.[2] The new board retained all previous powers, duties, and appointing procedures. By 1910, port interests realized that, to retain its competitive position, Boston needed improved and expanded port facilities. In that year, the legislature appropriated $3 million for the Board of Harbor and Land Commissioners to purchase necessary land in East Boston for a railroad line and to construct whatever piers or wharves were required in the area.[3]

The board could actually do little, however, to counter all the complex developments, in particular the rail rate situation, that were buffeting the Port of Boston. It was soon apparent that these adverse circumstances demanded more attention than the part-time statewide commissioners could spare and more statutory power than they could wield. Any supplemental body would need the authority to go beyond maintenance and supervision and concentrate solely on the administration and development of the Port of Boston. Hence, in 1911, "An Act Relative to the Development of the Port of Boston" established a new board in addition to the Board of Harbor and Land Commissioners, known as the Directors of the Port of Boston, the city's first real port authority as now understood.[4] The four members, three appointed by the governor and one appointed by the mayor of Boston, served three-year terms. Each director received an annual salary of $1,000, but the full-time chairman, designated by the governor, received $15,000 per year. The directors were given unprecedented power; they were given charge of all the Commonwealth's Boston harbor property and delegated the power to take, by purchase or eminent domain with the consent of the governor and council, other property and easements they considered necessary. While exemptions from eminent domain were granted to private owners who planned construction of new port facilities, the directors were given broad power to take any land necessary for connecting rail lines to port terminals. The importance of the railroads to port commerce was further reflected in the provisions to grade and surface railroad locations and provide track connections serving the piers to any railroad reaching the area. The directors could construct any piers or other public works and equip them with fireproof sheds, railway tracks, cranes, machinery, and other accommodations. They were empowered to administer all terminals under state control, set rules and regulations, and charge "reasonable" rates for the use of the facilities. They were allowed to lease out, for up to twenty years, wharves, piers, sheds, warehouses, and other facilities. The income from these facilities was paid into the general treasury of the Commonwealth.

Equal in importance to these administrative functions was the directive to make and execute plans for the comprehensive development of the harbor, including:

> . . . adequate piers, capable of accommodating the largest vessels, and in connection with such piers, suitable highways, waterways, railroad connections and storage yards, and sites for warehouses and industrial establishments.[5]

The directors were to report to the legislature on these plans and recommend any new legislation needed to implement them. They were allocated $50 thousand for salaries and studies and $9 million from the sale of state bonds for other expenses. Massachusetts had realized the fact that a strong, dynamic, well-financed administration was necessary for the Port of Boston to compete with the other North Atlantic ports and develop rather than dissipate its maritime commerce.

In 1914, the directors were reduced to three, to be appointed only by the governor.[6] They all received an annual salary of $6,000, and all members were required to devote full time to port activities. Furthermore, the need for solicitation of exports from the Midwest prompted an appropriation of $10,000 for a publicity bureau to extoll the virtues of the Port. This legislative revision increased the powers of the directors and gave added impetus for improved port facilities. By 1915, the directors had invested $3.5 million in improvements, including the construction of the 1,200-foot-long Commonwealth Pier, touted as "the greatest passenger and freight pier in the world."[7] Boston remained the fifth largest port in the world in total tonnage—behind New York, London, Hamburg, and Rotterdam—despite rapidly declining exports.

In 1916, however, port adminstration was weakened when the Directors of the Port of Boston and the Board of Harbor and Land Commissioners were abolished, and the Massachusetts Commission on Waterways and Public Lands was established.[8] The new agency assumed the powers, duties, and obligations of the previous boards, and professional superintendents of commerce and engineering were appointed. Nonetheless, the autonomy and effectiveness of the Port's administration were seriously weakened by its integration, once again, into a statewide agency.

This approach continued until 1919, when, under a general reorganization of the Commonwealth's executive and administrative functions, the Commission on Waterways and Public Lands was transferred to the new Department of Public Works.[9] There, the task of harbor management was assumed by the Division of Waterways headed by two full-time associate commissioners with annual salaries of $6,000.

While the steady decline of Boston's relative commercial status may have been inexorable, diluted port adminstration did not help matters. While Boston's total tonnage did increase, it did so at a much slower rate than that of competing ports. Furthermore, critical exports declined drastically from 1,256,892 tons in 1910 to 338,779 tons in 1925.[10]

In response to this trend, the autonomous Boston Port Authority (BPA) was established in 1929.[11] It consisted of five unpaid members, two appointed by the governor and three appointed by the mayor of Boston. For the first ten years, the expenses of the board were paid by the city of Boston and were limited to $50,000 per year. Later, the Commonwealth shared these expenses with the city. The BPA's powers were severely circumscribed, leaving all management functions in the Division of Waterways. It's limited role was to "investigate any and all matters relating to the port of Boston" and, with the assent and approval of the mayor, to

. . . initiate or participate in any rate proceedings, or any hearings or investigations concerning the port of Boston before any other body or official.[12]

The BPA was set up as an advisory rather than operational body. Handicapped by lack of funds and power, it could do little except devise plans and issue reports to combat the Port's commercial stagnation. To the persistent dilemma of an export shortage were added an escalating cost structure, deteriorating facilities, labor disputes, and a general lethargy towards the Port's worsening condition and its likely destiny. Boston lost an increasing amount of business to its North Atlantic competitors, especially New York. Even the trend of increasing total tonnage was reversed; exacerbated by the Depression, it dropped from 18,009,186 tons in 1929 to 15,739,926 tons in 1936. Exports fared even worse, as usual; they dropped from 303,120 tons in 1929 to 166,090 tons in 1933 and increased only to 312,410 tons in 1936.[13] While applauding the Boston Port Authority for the "splendid work" it had done—such as discovering and calling attention to the fact that Boston was nearer than Los Angeles to the Panama Canal—a legislative study commission in 1938 succinctly summarized the situation:

This Board up to the present time has been more or less helpless to correct certain evils which exist at the Port and concerning which there is a general opinion that if the Port of Boston is to progress and is to be a thriving port they must be eliminated.[14]

Unfortunately, the study commission felt the BPA would lose its independence and neutrality if it were given sufficient operational power and funding to compete with private enterprise. It concurred with the attitude that the BPA's appropriate role was advisory and saw salvation through implementing its sole recommendation that two additional members be added to the board to stimulate "Port enthusiasm" and "Port spirit," the lack of which it surmised to be the major cause of the Port's ills. Although the BPA was so enlarged, the study commission may as well have recommended a booster club.

In fact, though, a new interest in the Port did emerge very shortly; World War II, however, was more responsible for it than any legislative prescription. Despite the serious disruption of steamship services and the normal flow of commerce, the prosperous war years saw a renovation of port facilities. Under the prevailing emergency conditions, the efficient allocation and routing of ships and coordination of port activities demonstrated to local leaders the advantages of concentrating certain maritime activities in the hands of a few responsible officials. Moreover, the unprecedented movement of men and materials impressed many with the Port of Boston's stature as a principal national asset during wartime.

Ironically, this parallels the historical United States view since the beginning of the nineteenth century towards its merchant marine. Only during wartime has the government recognized the absolute requisite for national security of a large efficient merchant fleet. This has always stimulated a crash construction program. In the ensuing peace, however, the cycle begins again as the American merchant marine deteriorates while the country's waterborne commerce is carried in foreign vessels.

Nevertheless, interest in the Port was revived with a view towards a commensurate commercial role for it in times of peace. This new attitude was reflected in a legislative report in 1943:

There is a new interest in the Port in important transportation circles both abroad and in this country. Boston is one of the great war ports of the United States and the United Nations. We believe it can become one of the great peacetime ports as well.[15]

During the war, various civic groups and maritime interests devoted serious efforts to port studies. They found the Boston Port Authority, jointly operated by the city and state with limited powers, personnel, and finances, inadequate if Boston was to prosper as a seaport. Their basic recommendation was that it be replaced by a stronger, more autonomous authority that, as a state agency, would be responsible for all phases of port administration.

As a result, in 1945 the primarily advisory Boston Port Authority was abolished and a new Port of Boston Authority (PBA) was established.[16] It consisted of five unpaid members appointed solely by the governor for five-year terms. The operative head was a full-time salaried director with the authority to hire such experts as commerce counsels, traffic solicitors, and rate experts. The PBA was closely modeled after the Directors of the Port of Boston, and its extensive powers, duties, and obligations were nearly identical to those of the earlier body. It was to investigate all matters related to the Port, plan for port development, and exercise the licensing power over harbor projects previously vested in the Department of Public Works.

The only significant differences between the PBA and the earlier directors were in the areas of facility construction and financing. The PBA was required to secure a minimum lease contract for any proposed facility before it was constructed with a bond issue. Furthermore, bonds issued by the Commonwealth for port construction were limited to $15 million and were to be specifically designated as Boston Harbor Facilities Loans. Finally, the PBA's finances were further distinguished from the state's general fiscal structure by the establishment of a Port of Boston Fund, into which all port revenues were placed and from which legislative appropriations for port expenses were derived.

The Authority soon developed an ambitious "Port of Boston Master Plan" for a coordinated development of port, trucking, and rail facilities into an efficiently integrated transportation system that would serve an expanded tributary area including states north of the Ohio River, west of the Mississippi, and the Canadian Provinces. To implement this plan, by 1950, the PBA and private enterprises had invested $21,158,857 in harbor improvements and port facilities, carefully planned along a functional pattern to allow rapid interchange of cargo between highway and rail carriers and ships.[17] Hoosac Pier No. 1 was the first general cargo terminal constructed in Boston in 37 years. It was followed by the construction of the Mystic Terminal and East Boston Pier No. 1. A Division for Promotion and Solicitation was established in 1947 with branch offices in New York, Washington, and Chicago; it successfully acquired for the Port significant food exports under the Foreign Aid Program (Marshall Plan). An active Public Relations Division was effective in improving public opinion

of the Port, and the PBA helped to maintain sufficiently good labor management relations to avert any major disruptions. By 1949, the Port could boast a
25 percent increase in total tonnage over 1937, the last normal prewar year.

In 1953, the name of the Port of Boston Authority was changed to the Port
of Boston Commission (PBC) and an advisory council was established.[18] The
council consisted of the mayor of Boston and twenty representatives from industrial, shipping, trade, civic, labor, and transportation organizations. A year
later, the legislature appropriately transferred the responsibility for dredging
tidelands, shore protection, and other related matters to the Division of Waterways of the Department of Public Works, thus allowing the PBC to concentrate
exclusively on administration and development.

Unfortunately, despite all this attention, the Port of Boston did not prosper
as was hoped. Total tonnage showed no appreciable increase after 1949, while
the import-export imbalance worsened, not withstanding the increased costs of
solicitation and publicity. In 1949, Boston ranked 37th in exports among U.S.
ports. Meanwhile, rival North Atlantic ports were increasing both their total and
export tonnage. General figures for dry cargo exports in 1954 reflect Boston's
declining competitive position: New York, 4,700,000 tons; Baltimore,
3,500,000 tons; Philadelphia, 2,000,000 tons; and Boston, 281,000 tons.[19] Even
minor ports — like Toledo, Sandusky, and Port Sulphur, Louisiana — exceeded
Boston in tonnage of dry cargo exports. The character of Boston's imports was
equally discouraging. It was estimated that the arrival of one general cargo ship
represented a total income of $100,000 to Boston. Dominated by such bulk
commodities as petroleum, coal, and sugar, which are handled through private
facilities, the vast majority of vessels arriving at the Port generated only minimal
revenues.

By the mid-1950s, there was growing concern about not only the seaport,
but Boston's entire commercial future. It was felt that, without bold or radical
steps, Boston could never expect to assume its proper place as a thriving metropolitan center. A critical component of this "New Boston" revival was the future
expansion and operation of the area's land, sea, and air transportation facilities.
Consolidated administration of these components in a self-sustaining authority
operated on sound business principles was believed to be the only approach to
counter increasing competition and strained financial resources. International
adoption of various modifications of such a system had been expanding for some
time:

The delegation of port administration to a non-stock, non-profit public corporate agency created by statute with a legal personality of its own, the right to
hold property, make contracts, adopt budgets, employ its own personnel, and
function with considerable financial autonomy, is a development of the past
half century which has spread to an increasingly larger segment of the ports of
the world.[20]

In 1948, the management of the two state-owned airports, Logan International and the much smaller, civil/military Hanscom Field, was placed in the the State Airport Management Board. It gradually became obvious that both this board and the Port of Boston Commission were severely handicapped in operating their facilities as business enterprises by their inclusion in the general structure of the state government. Impediments seemed inevitable if such bodies were subjected to competition for general state funds during times of scarce resources, jurisdiction divided among several state officers and legislative committees, and the political requisites of patronage, pork barrels, and partisan influence. Progress was difficult when such bodies were enmeshed in

. . . the intricate and complex web of legislative and executive controls over policy, management, budgeting, financing, personnel and building construction, all of which are desirable and necessary for activities of the regular state departments and agencies.[21]

The consequences of such a situation were manifest in the operation of the state's transport facilities: rigid and inflexible management; constrained decision making and an inability to take fast action; lack of coordinated and long-range planning for an integrated transportation system; and insufficient funds for necessary promotion and capital investment. The "New Boston" could never compete successfully if burdened with such a management and financial structure. A general movement for political reform at the time reinforced this rationale for a new body disentangled from the state government system. A strong reaction had developed against the political corruption that tainted many public activities, and there was a growing demand for restoring "clean government" throughout the state. This atmosphere of righteous reform enhanced the appeal of a port agency that would be above traditional political manipulation.

The other major incentive for a self-supporting authority was the Commonwealth's deplorable fiscal condition. The state was in a financial crisis with over an $800 million debt and a recently lowered credit rating. While there was a compelling need for an aggressive, forward-looking action program, money was not at hand for the required promotion and expansion of the state's commerce. Moreover, while the over $100 million public investment in the two airports and the seaport had to be protected, these facilities had become an unbearable burden on the taxpayers. The 1957 difference between revenues and operating costs for all facilities was $3,890,178. From 1949 to 1955, the accumulated deficit for the Port of Boston was $6,372,857.60; that of Logan Airport was $28,022,105.26; and that of Hanscom Field was $366,667.57.[22] There was mounting pressure from state legislators from the suburbs and the western part of the state to relieve nonusers of this additional tax burden.

In glaring contrast to this sad state of affairs was the thriving transport system of Boston's nearest competitor. The self-sufficient Port of New York

Authority, established in 1921, had already invested $0.5 billion dollars in facilities and was embarked on a development program with another $0.5 billion, $140 million of which was earmarked for marine terminals. In fact, the Director of the Port of New York Authority defined most clearly the ethos of the international adoption of such bodies:

A governmental business corporation set up outside of the normal structure of government so that it can apply continuity, business efficiency and elastic management to the construction or operation of a self-supporting or revenue-producing enterprise.[23]

Boston's rival ports had already recognized the value of such a management scheme and similar authorities were successfully operating in Philadelphia, Baltimore, Norfolk, New Orleans, and the St. Lawrence Seaway. Massachusetts had already witnessed the effectiveness of such an approach in the construction and operation of the Mystic River Bridge and had subsequently established the Massachusetts Turnpike Authority.

In the process of historical development even nearby political and economic units experience widely different rates of maturation. Thus, as New York was historically ripe for a new method of port management thirty-five years earlier, Boston's slower evolution resulted in a much later coincidence of its struggle to relieve its belabored transportation system and its capacity to commit itself to a new approach. After a prolonged period of experimentation without progress, Boston's day, in effect, had arrived. Despite heated legislative debate, the concept of a Massachusetts Port Authority had the support of organized labor, civic leaders, and, most importantly, the business community. An emergency bill survived twenty-eight amendments and the Commonwealth had a new "Authority." An across-the-board administrative, political, and fiscal reform of Boston's transport system was too appealing. The special legislative commission that studied and recommended the establishment of the new authority summarized the prevailing attitude:

It is a program that envisions large new construction and unlimited job opportunities. It is a program which has for its goal the highest and most efficient use of our major traffic, terminal, transportation, port and airport facilities. It is a program of tax relief for the Commonwealth. It is a program that could light the spark for the economic resurgence of an entire community.[24]

Under Chapter 465 of the Acts of 1956, the Massachusetts Port Authority (Massport) was established, to become operative in 1959. The original legislation was filed in 1955 by Governor Christian A. Herter, but it did not include the seaport. Powerfully opposed, it was rejected by the legislature. A recesss study commission was appointed to report on the matter, and its basic recommendations were embodied in the final enabling act. Of the seven Massport members

appointed by the governor for seven-year terms, one had to be a labor repre-
sentative, and not more than four could be from the same political party. The
"body politic and corporate" created was nominally placed in the Department
of Public Works, but was not

> . . . subject to the supervision or regulation of the department of public works or
> of any department, commission, board, bureau or agency of the Common-
> wealth.[25]

Massport constituted a "public instrumentality" and the exercise of its powers
was deemed to be "the performance of an essential government function."

All state properties in the Port of Boston, Logan International Airport,
Hanscom Field, and the Mystic River Bridge were transfered to Massport, and it
was granted expansive general powers, including those formerly held by the Port
of Boston Commission. It was authorized to control, operate, and maintain all
the properties given it, and to fix, revise, and collect tolls, rates, fees, rentals, and
other charges for their use. It could establish rules and regulations for these facilities and construct and acquire new ones. Massport was given the power to acquire, by purchase or eminent domain, public and private property, easements,
or other interests in land. It was to devise a plan for the development, improvement, and handling of commerce in the metropolitan area, including the construction and operation of a trade and transportation center. It could appear in
its own behalf before boards, commissions, departments, or agencies; apply for
and accept federal grants; enter into contracts and agreements; sue and be sued;
and initiate or participate in rate proceedings or any hearings or investigations
concerning the Port of Boston.

Though these powers were substantial, most pertaining to the Port had been
vested in previous authorities. The keystone to Massport's coordinated administration of all of Boston's transportation components was the autonomy that
only its new fiscal structure could allow. Massport's self-sufficiency was intended
to be derived from its power to issue its own revenue bonds, payable solely from
user-charges at its facilities and to borrow money in anticipation of these issues.
Since the Authority's operations were "essential government functions," its
bonds as well as its property were exempt from federal and state taxes, making
them especially attractive and allowing their sale at an interest rate of about 2
percent lower than the going market rate. Massport did not need the consent of
any other state or city body to issue these bonds, which neither constituted a
debt nor pledged the "faith and credit" of the Commonwealth or any political
subdivision. The Authority's financial independence was hoped to stop the drain
on the Commonwealth's treasury, reimburse the state for previous investments
in the seaport and airports, and generate the money necessary for operating expenses and future construction and improvement of transportation facilities.

The Commonwealth transferred to Massport its extensive port holdings,
including Castle Island, the Boston Army Base, the Boston Fish Pier, Common-

wealth Pier, the Mystic Piers, the Hoosac Piers, and the East Boston Piers. This was not a total giveaway, however, since the state sought to recoup some of its losses from these facilities. When the airport properties were transferred, Massport had to pay the state the aggregate principal amounts of all previous bonds issued and cash payments made for airport improvement, amounting to $20,972, 151. Furthermore, the state's earlier investment in port facilities was to be gradually repaid by the yearly net revenues from port properties after overhead and construction expenses and principal and interest requirements. By the year 2019, a total of $17,057,321 was to be returned to the state for these seaport holdings.

The critical component that allowed the new authority to meet these initial obligations was the Mystic River Bridge, a crucial highway link to Boston's populous North Shore and the entire northern New England area. In 1958, the bridge enjoyed the traffic of over 20 million toll-paying motor vehicles. The Mystic River Bridge Authority, established in 1946 to construct and operate the toll bridge, was not only self-supporting but generated an annual excess of revenues over operating costs of about $3.5 million. This abundance of user fees would have retired the bridge's bonds and allowed it to become toll free by the late 1970s. However, the establishment of Massport altered this arrangement. Massport was allowed to refinance the Mystic River Bridge revenue bonds. It thus acquired the immediate payment for the airport facilities and the use of the proven, long-range revenue generating abilities of the bridge as a secure, initial credit base for new bond issues to finance the operation and expansion of other facilities. In February 1959, Massport floated its first revenue bond issue of $71,750,000 at 4.75 percent interest. From this, it paid for the airport properties, retired $22,160,500 of the Mystic River Bridge bonds, and acquired a comfortable bit of capital with which to start its operation. When the other facilities were able to turn a profit, the "closed-system" nature of Massport's financial structure was strengthened and it had no difficulty floating additional bonds.

This scheme seemed to satisfy everyone except those bridge proponents who had been anticipating the toll-free era as a fitting reward to the Massachusetts taxpayer and a monument to that rare species, the efficient public project. Otherwise, all parties seemed satisfied. The Supreme Judicial Court, when asked for its advisory opinion on the enabling act, found the new body, despite its corporate appearance, to be in no sense a private or business corporation:

It has no stockholders; no person can derive a profit through its operation. Only the public is to be benefited.[26]

The Court deemed that, not only was the bill constitutional, but its fiscal provisions were

... necessary parts of the whole enterprise conceived and intended for the maintenance and extension of great improvements wholly for the public benefit.[27]

Everyone seemed to win. Massport was handed administrative and financial power and a package of facilities worth about $237 million; the Commonwealth was rid of a drain on its strained fiscal resources and could look forward to eventually recovering at least $38 million of its past investments; and the public, relieved of a tax burden, could await the commercial renaissance that the vigorous, dynamic, and autonomous Massachusetts Port Authority would usher in through its air terminals, piers, and toll booths.

# 3

The Constitution of the Port:
Trade Imbalance and
Petroleum

*Between the idea*
*And the reality*
*Between the notion*
*And the act*
*Falls the Shadow*
　　　　　　T.S. Eliot

Despite the ministrations of the various boards and authorities, the Port of
Boston inexorably declined. Its economic viability has been questioned and
there is uncertainty as to whether it can emerge from its present state of stagnation. Behind this deterioration has been a complex of numerous and interrelated
factors, many of which have origins in the distant past. The resolution or persist-
ence of these problems will determine the Port's future. Recently, under the
aegis of the Massachusetts Port Authority, there has been a more positive and
concerted assault upon some of the principal dilemmas that impede the Port's
progressive development. The following chapters will deal with some of the chief
components in this process, focusing on their present impact and the efforts
being made to accommodate or alter them.

## Trade Imbalance

Although the individual ailments the Port has endured are not unique to Boston,
in combination they have disproportionately exacerbated the principal malady
that has afflicted the Port for most of its history: a crippling trade imbalance.
Basic economics dictates that no one except the crew makes money when a ship,
having discharged its cargo, is forced to sail empty from a port. A fair balance of
trade prevents this to the greatest possible extent. Severe imbalances, however,
are a chronic condition of seaborne general cargo trades and have resulted in
concentrations of freight movement in large, regional ports in order to secure the
optimum equilibrium in the flow of traffic.[1]

An acceptable trade balance, therefore, is a prerequisite for a healthy, growing general seaport. It alone can attract major shipping lines which offer the necessary frequent and regular general cargo service schedules. This in turn attracts
even more freight, both import and export, and also those industries dependent
on cheap waterborne transportation. These scheduled general cargo services not

only enhance a port's competitive stature, but also generate maximum port revenues. It has been estimated that North Atlantic ports generate $16 to their respective state economies for every ton of general cargo handled.[2] The traditional sources of these revenues are the purchases of stores, water, and bunkers; tugboat and harbor pilot fees; and pier charges and stevedore wages. Even with Boston's small general cargo traffic, this means about $30 million a year to Massachusetts. Bulk cargoes, both liquid and dry, usually use private facilities and so generate only minimal port revenues.

Boston's excess of inbound over outbound traffic evolved as the Port was gradually confined to servicing only the New England economic configuration. The extent and nature of the hinterland served, not necessarily limited to contiguous areas, shapes the size and character of a port. Specialized ports may develop to handle the predominant product of a large region — as Melbourne, Capetown, and Santos have done for wheat, minerals, and coffee. Great world ports, such as Rotterdam and New York, thrive because of the extent and diversity of the industrial, agricultural, and commercial needs of their hinterlands. Boston's initial hinterland was probably artificially large due to its early establishment as a major port, the physical limitations of the young nation, and the manageable competition from other North Atlantic ports. It truly served as an entrepôt for the entire country and could draw on the western regions for import and export traffic. The makeup of this hinterland was destined to change, however; by a gradual but inexorable attrition, the Port was restricted to a more immediate hinterland. Some of the main forces behind this process were seen in the Port's history: geographical disadvantages; increased competition; shifting centers of population, consumption, and production; and a discriminatory cost structure.

To appreciate the ultimate effects of such a restriction, the present waterborne commerce market areas of Boston can be divided into four natural groupings. Since inland carrier rates played a critical role in the Port's decline, they are appropriate criteria for this delimitation. The four groupings are:

1. *The Boston port area and immediate hinterland.* This includes Rhode Island and eastern Massachusetts.
2. *The balance of Boston's lower inland rate area.* This covers the rest of New England except three counties in Connecticut. This and the above area are the only areas in which Boston enjoys a rail and truck rate advantage.
3. *The equal rate area.* This includes, roughly, Ohio, Indiana, Michigan, and the metropolitan areas of Milwaukee, Chicago, Pittsburgh, Buffalo, Rochester, and Syracuse. No other North Atlantic port enjoys a rail rate advantage over Boston for this area, but several have lower truck rates.
4. *The balance of the country.* In these areas, Boston's rail and truck rates would be higher than those of at least one other major port.

As to be expected, the vast majority of the Port's import and export traffic is generated in the port area and immediate hinterland, with a much smaller amount coming from the rest of New England. The equal rail rate area and the rest of the country are responsible for only minimal traffic through Boston. This is demonstrated by general cargo import traffic shown in Table 3-1.

**Table 3-1**
**General Cargo Import Traffic**

| Area of destination | Percentage of all Boston General cargo imports |
| --- | --- |
| Port area and immediate hinterland | 79 |
| Rest of New England | 14 |
| Midwest equal rail rate area | 4 |
| Balance of the country | 3 |

*Source:* Rowland and MacNeal, *Port of Boston Waterborne Commerce Market and Development Requirements,* New York, 1964, p. 16.

The limits of Boston's hinterland have been closely defined. The character of this area, however, is more responsible than its extent for the Port's condition. Lacking resources, New England is barren of the bulk exports needed to fill a ship's hold. The basic economic structure, determined by nature, necessity, and enterprise, has traditionally demanded huge amounts of imported food, raw materials, and fuel. With the early exception of the codfish and the later exception of a biannual apple crop, the region has offered no consistent, indigenous export base. Manufactures, in small lot shipments entailing time- and profit-consuming excessive handling, did not prove to be the much needed and long hoped for export medium.

This pattern continues today. Even dry bulk imports pale before the complete domination of petroleum products which the area relies upon to produce its power, feed its factories, heat its homes, and fuel its motor vehicles and aircraft. Future industrial development and population growth, the "energy crisis" notwithstanding, are expected to result in a faster acceleration of this consumption rate around Boston.[3] The Port's major role has become primarily that of the terminus of a life-line of raw materials from foreign and domestic sources.

The New England states have a smaller than average proportion of the basic materials industries — petroleum, coal, and primary metals — that generate bulk exports. They do have a far greater than average proportion of paper, textile, leather, instrument, machinery, rubber, and plastic industries which produce expensive but low volume goods.[4] The trend of declining general cargo tonnage in the Port will continue as specialized construction of small components, such as the electrical machinery industry, becomes an ever more important sector of the local economy.[5] It goes without saying that most of these products are consumed domestically and that, of those intended for foreign commerce, 85 percent are exported through New York, while 50 percent of the area's industrial foreign import needs also flow through New York.

The question remains: what has been done to alleviate this dilemma? Boston's import-export imbalance is an old problem and efforts to abate it were initiated early. The thrust of these efforts has been the solicitation of shippers, industries, railroads, and steamship lines, a practice that has become the backbone of most major competitive ports. Since 1914, solicitation programs had been executed by the Directors of the Port of Boston, the Boston Port Authority, and the Port of Boston Commissioners. Notwithstanding increased expenditures, they were generally ineffective.

The Massachusetts Port Authority inherited a quandary not of its own making, whose roots — the basic economic structure of New England — it was powerless to attack directly. Solicitation, however, was one of the prime responsibilities assigned it. Massport's early policy in attempting to attract new commerce, especially export shipments, fluctuated in seemingly contradictory fashion. This apparent inconsistency makes sense, however, if one assumes that the way was being prepared, long before public articulation, for Massport's "master plan" for the total containerization of the Port, a strategy so intangible, poorly defined, and haphazardly pursued that it might be better termed a state of mind.

Massport undertook an initially successful campaign to encourage industrial development along Boston's waterfront in order to increase bulk imports and hopefully generate some much needed dry bulk exports. At the time, Boston was seen by many observers to be a potentially important specialized port for bulk imports.[6] In the early 1960s, progress was marked by the establishment of the Eastern Gas and Fuel Associates facility for handling molten liquid sulphur, an American Sugar Company plant, and three cement companies — Universal Atlas Cement, Marquette Cement, and Atlantic Cement — with combined storage facilities for 222,500 barrels.

Little more was done after this, however, and Massport was criticized for slackening its pace and not developing and implementing a comprehensive plan for Boston's commercial future. In fact, in 1973, the Port lost one of its oldest bulk industries when the Revere Sugar Refinery in Charlestown closed down, depriving Boston of three sugar ships a month.[7] Massport's port director blamed the lack of gains after this initial flush of success on inadequate site locations and the 7.5 percent Massachusetts income tax on business corporations, the highest in the country.[8] Other ports, however, exhibited more persistent efforts to establish integrated industrial centers similar to Europort (Rotterdam). This is evidenced by such developments as the Port of Oakland Industrial Park and the River Gate Industrial District of the Port of Portland. In retrospect, it seems that Massport's waning enthusiasm for such industries was as much inspired by its vague conviction that the Port's future lay in containers and not bulk. Boston already possessed sufficient bulk traffic and Massport correctly recognized that additional cargoes would generate little revenue for it and most other port interests.

This reasoning also helps to explain Massport's reaction to the possibility of renewed grain exports. Boston found rail rate parity was not a panacea. In 1956, the Port of Boston Authority, joined by the local railroads and New York port interests, began a legal drive to remove the discriminatory rail rate differentials; the effort was carried on by Massport. In 1960, the Interstate Commerce Commission (ICC) refused to equalize rates with the "Southern tier" of North Atlantic ports, citing the greater inland distances to Boston and New York.[9] This decision was appealed to the Federal District Court in Boston, where it was argued that Norfolk was only thirty-eight miles closer to the Central Freight Association territory than Boston. The court overturned the ICC decision, finding that "the Commission's decision is erroneous in law and lacks the rational basis to uphold it."[10] In 1963, the U.S. Supreme Court, divided evenly, four to four, let stand the District Court's ruling.[11] The eight-year struggle had cost Massport $150,000, but the Port's burden of eighty-six years had been lifted.

There was understandable jubilation in Boston. The President of the Greater Boston Chamber of Commerce felt the ruling to mean "the rejuvenation of Boston's window on the world."[12] The Mayor called it "one of the most important judicial decisions in almost a century, a major victory for Boston which will now have the opportunity of again taking its position as a major world port."[13] The Executive Director of Massport heralded it as

. . . a potentially tremendous benefit to Boston and the entire area. We now have an opportunity to expand our marketing area, now limited to New England, as far west as the Mississippi.[14]

A $25,000 sales campaign was to be fully organized and undertaken to beat the bushes for Midwest bulk and general cargo.

Feelings were high that, for Boston to regain its former status as a grain exporter, it needed improved rail service from the west based on large, self-discharging freight cars that could transform a trainload automatically into a shipload, the construction of modern silos and facilities, and the commitment of a large exporter. Nothing materialized, however. Massport was honestly unable to find a private investor willing to risk the establishment of expensive new grain-handling facilities in the Port. Shortly after its invigorating promise of an ambitious grain crusade, Massport was roundly criticized for allowing the New York Central Railroad to prematurely abrogate its lease and shut down the Port's last grain elevator in East Boston. In 1966, Boston lost its share of a 3-million-ton emergency wheat shipment to India because it had no operating grain elevators. At the time, a Department of Agriculture spokesman could truthfully say that "Boston is not in the grain business anymore."[15] While established traffic patterns through other North Atlantic ports were admittedly difficult to break, Massport's solicitation efforts were minimal and half-hearted, including an entertaining but not very productive color-sound movie, presumptuously entitled, "The Port of Boston — Gateway to the West."[16] Massport's actions seemed to belie its earlier words.

Behind this contradiction seems to have been the Authority's deliberate policy to avoid the futility of a frontal assault on the St. Lawrence Seaway. Though grain traffic through all U.S. ports, including Boston, had increased substantially in the postwar period, after its opening in 1959, the Seaway quickly developed a stranglehold on much of the bulk grain exports from the Great Lakes region. While it diverted some trade from all U.S. North Atlantic ports, it in effect destroyed Boston and New York as grain shippers, while the "Southern tier" continued to thrive. (See Table 3-2.)

Massport's assessment of the grain situation proved wise. Utilizing shipload lots, the Seaway offered lower freight rates because of a longer waterborne route. Not only was the inland carriage cheaper, but the Canadian Shipping Conference quoted lower ocean freight tariffs than the American Shipping Conference which governed Boston's traffic. Moreover, the subsidized Canadian National Railroad quoted cheaper rates to St. John's and Halifax than did the American lines to U.S. coastal ports, if a full rail carriage was necessitated by the Seaway's freezing over. Boston was only treated to an occasional spillover from these Canadian ports and its grain traffic was reduced to a trickle.

Massport recognized the threat that this new competitor represented and filed early protests against the federal promotion of the St. Lawrence Seaway. In 1962, the Executive Director stated that

. . . the promotion of the St. Lawrence Seaway is not a responsibility of the Federal government. The Seaway ports should shoulder their own responsibilities as do other ports of the United States.[17]

This agitation was of no avail. By 1972, total cargo traffic on the Seaway reached a record 53.7 million tons. Twenty-one and a half million tons of grain accounted for 47 percent of the 45.9-million-ton total bulk traffic. Windfalls, such as the U.S.–Soviet Shipping Agreement of 1972, increased the normal flow of wheat, corn, soybeans, and barley through the Seaway. In the same year, the Seaway also handled 7.9 million tons of general cargo and 12.6 million tons of iron ore.[18]

The Seaway's full potential may not yet be fully realized. The U.S. Congress has funded a three-year Navigation Season Extension Demonstration Program. If

Table 3-2
**Foreign Exports of Corn, Wheat, and Soybeans Through U.S. North Atlantic Ports**
(short tons)

| Year | Boston | New York | Philadelphia | Baltimore | Hampton Roads | Total foreign exports of corn, wheat, and soybeans, through all U.S. ports | Grain exports as percent of total foreign exports through all U.S. ports |
|---|---|---|---|---|---|---|---|
| 1959 | 323,521 | 420,621 | 534,642 | 1,215,914 | 2,425,377 | 20,422,939 | 7.5 |
| 1969 | 10 | 28,246 | 365,387 | 451,857 | 2,666,759 | 37,982,209 | 6.6 |
| 1972 | 71 | 18,248 | 1,360,667 | 2,197,008 | 4,277,551 | 60,828,800 | 8.9 |

*Source:* U.S. Army Corps of Engineers, *Waterborne Commerce of the United States, Calendar Years 1959, 1969, 1972* (Washington, D.C.: U.S. Government Printing Office, 1960, 1970, 1973), parts 1 and 5.

successful, the year-round use of the Great Lakes and the St. Lawrence Seaway through the development of sophisticated ice booms seems imminent.[19]

Boston's loss of grain shipments meant more than just losing the $4.24 that each bushel was estimated to contribute to the local economy. An industry observer noted that

... the large grain movements, which Boston formerly had, served to generate other cargoes. Since grain needs very rapid movement, the port which can provide such service acquires a favorable reputation which helps to attract other commodities.[20]

With just the opposite reputation, the Port has had to hobble along with exports of scrap iron and tallow.

Along with this pessimism about competing with the St. Lawrence Seaway, there seem to have been other motives to Massport's behavior. Besides the differential decision, 1963 also marked the ascendancy of Edward King as the new Executive Director of Massport. A strong and dynamic leader, he gave first priority to an immediate and vigorous development program for Logan Airport, but he also seems to have been committed to an as yet inchoate design for the long-term containerization of the seaport, which unfortunately had to be temporarily deferred. Thus, as with bulk industries, grain exports may have appeared dispensable and even incompatible with Boston's containerized future, barely worth the effort to pry them from the Seaway's grip. This notion is supported by the interesting fact that Massport has recently undertaken a small solicitation drive for Midwest grain and even popcorn, now that such traditional bulk shipments are being increasingly containerized.

There are indications, however, that Boston's chances for handling Midwest grain might be somewhat improved in the future. One possible opportunity may result from changing economics in the grain industry as a whole. It has been suggested to Massport that some shifting market patterns may indicate a modification of the existing distribution system and make it once again advantageous to use ports such as Boston for grain storage and transatlantic shipment. The second factor that may redound in Boston's favor is reduced utilization of the St. Lawrence Seaway, despite aforementioned efforts to extend its navigational season. Ships, especially the new class of Ore/Bulk/Oil combination vessels, are fast outgrowing the Seaway and traffic seems decidedly on the decline. The Seaway's locks restrict passage to ships drawing up to 25.5 feet, limiting loads to 27,000 tons for lakers and to only 10,000 tons for oceangoing vessels due to their different shape. This is imposing severe restraints on ex-Lake grain shipments via the Seaway as the expanding O/B/O fleet demonstrates the same rapid growth in individual vessel size as have supertankers.

Whether or not these two developments might actually have significant effects on the general movement of American grain, they are having no effect on

Massport's prognosis. The Authority still believes Boston has no future in grain and that basic economics argue against any efforts to pursue one; it sees as ill-advised any plans or investments in anticipation of substantially altered flow patterns in the grain industry. Massport's rationale is based principally on its conviction that the Gulf of Mexico will remain the nation's greatest grain export region and that the St. Lawrence Seaway no longer has any appreciable effect on shipping in Boston. A recent analysis of inland barge transportation makes Massport's assessment of the Gulf ports' grip on the grain business seem realistic rather than defeatist.[21] Barge transportation on the inland waterways currently represents the largest segment of domestic shipping and one of the fastest growing transport modes in the United States. It is both cheap and efficient; the tonnage of individual tows is rapidly increasing, while costs have been stabilized at a level approximating that of fifty years ago. Not only is the cost of shipping by barge only one-fifth that of shipping by rail, but the slow speed of barges allows them to function as great floating warehouses, helping to control market flow. With more than one half of the nation's barge traffic centered on the Mississippi River system and a large percentage of this made up of grain shipments, Massport's view of the Gulf's hegemony seems valid.

While it might be argued that, with Boston's limited export resources, even the incremental benefit of reviving a modest grain business would merit further study and a possible response, Massport's efforts will continue to revolve around containers and dismiss grain.

Massport's campaign to attract regional shippers of general cargo presently using New York is part of this total program of containerization and will be discussed later. Suffice it to say here that its efforts to sell Boston as a cheaper and faster shipping center than New York, for both containerized and break-bulk cargo, have been successful in New England, and inroads have even been made in New York state. Massport, in its conviction that most of the area's high-value–low-bulk manufactures are ideally suited for containerization, must consider, however, the entrenched habits of local shippers using New York and the increasing competition for this freight from the burgeoning air cargo business. Furthermore, it may be short-sighted to overlook the broader export potential in the Midwest and delay intense solicitation efforts in the region, which, led by Illinois, is presently the nation's largest source of both agricultural and industrial exports.

## Petroleum

Most bulk traffic requires specialized private facilities, generates only minimal port revenues, and does not necessarily enhance the status of a general cargo conference-liner seaport. Petroleum imports, however, dominate Boston's total tonnage and have provided its only really indispensable function: the Port of

Boston could justify itself solely as the terminus of an energy lifeline. Though fuel prices are certainly not low, cheap seaborne transport and Boston's proximity to the eastern Masssachusetts center of consumption, keep them from climbing even higher. There has been some resentment that New England, especially sensitive to environmental dangers, prefers to use imported petroleum products and thus preserves its coastline from the threat of crude oil terminals, offshore drilling, and refinery-industrial complexes. The area has not had the best of both worlds, however; during the peak of the 1973–1974 energy crisis, New England's external sources proved expensive and unreliable and the northeast states suffered the most acute fuel shortages. Some feel this situation could be even worse and that, without immediate and extensive improvements, Boston could be displaced as a major petroleum port. There is a demand not just for capital investment, but also for a comprehensive regional plan that genuinely considers environmental factors in integrating new facilities into an invaluable yet already strained coastal zone. Though the Port does not have a reputation of facile adaptation to technological developments and an impulsive stampede should be properly avoided, local sentiment for a while was less uncompromising and there is a possibility of a more realistic accommodation of some necessary evils.

The New England region has a historic and singular reliance on energy supplies from foreign and domestic sources inexpensively carried by the bulk trade. The area has no indigenous energy resources; relatively cold winters; a high degree of industrialization; a high population density, especially in eastern Massachusetts; and no pipeline system. Its imports fall into three categories of approximately equal size:

1. Gasoline and jet fuel.
2. Distillate fuel oils — #1 and #2 (home heating fuels) oils, kerosene, range oil, and diesel fuels.
3. Residual fuel oils — #5 and #6 fuel oils for utilities, industries, and bunkers for ships.

In recent years, the market for imported petroleum products had grown at an average rate of 1.3 percent per year.[22] Industrial development and population growth had been expected to result in a faster acceleration of the consumption rate, especially in the Boston area, but these projections may prove somewhat liberal given prevailing national consumption trends. Nevertheless, this general pattern of dependence should persist until at least 1985 but more probably the end of the century, even if recent efforts toward conservation, the search for new domestic sources, and the development of alternative sources are moderately successful.

New England's unique reliance on petroleum products as compared to the U.S. on a whole is shown in the Table 3-3.

Table 3–3
Petroleum Reliance, New England and the U.S.

|  | New England | United States |
|---|---|---|
| Percentage residential/commercial energy needs met by oil | 76 | 33 |
| Per capita consumption of distillate and residual fuel oil | 12.7 bbl | 3.3 bbl |

*Source:* Frederick R. Harris, Inc., *Feasibility Investigation: Massport Out-To-Sea Terminal System, Interim Report,* Boston, 1970, p. 12.

Massachusetts uses 52.2 percent of the entire New England oil consumption. Seventy-six percent of this, or over 40 percent of the entire regional supply, is consumed within fifty miles of Boston and is distributed from oil brought through the Port.[23] In 1972, Boston handled 22,838,239 tons of petroleum products.[24] This distribution arrangement is expected to continue in the future with whatever increases there may be in total New England flow passing through Boston. (See Table 3–4).

Practically all of New England's gasoline and distillate heating fuels originate in the Gulf of Mexico. Of the total supply about 55 percent is processed in the Gulf, 40 percent in the Pennsylvania-New Jersey refinery complex, and 5 percent in Puerto Rico and St. Croix. From these points, the refined products are transshipped by U.S. flag vessels to Boston where they constitute two-thirds of the Port's total petroleum tonnage. Since U.S. refineries prefer to use "cracking" processes to produce the more profitable gasoline and distillate heating fuels, New England relies upon foreign imports for its residual fuel oils. The primary source of supply is the Caribbean basin, with Venezuela, Trinidad, Aruba, and Curaçao accounting for 70 percent of the total. This oil is transported by foreign flag vessels and amounts to one-third of the Port's petroleum tonnage.

As with most U.S. ports, Boston's oil terminals have been unfortunately locked into the coventional Port. These inner-harbor terminals, located principally along the Chelsea Creek and the Mystic River, handle most of the Port's petroleum traffic. The complex access routes offer beam and depth restrictions, with mean low-water depths of 35 to 40 feet, and the location of these facilities presents time consuming turnaround problems.

Since petroleum products require special off-loading and storage, they have customarily been handled by private interests; hence in Boston, these private companies, rather than Massport, are responsible for the redundancy and unsatisfactory conditions of the terminals. At present, twenty-six facilities owned by fifteen companies handle 97.5 percent of all petroleum traffic in the Port.[25]

**Table 3–4**
**Regional Petroleum Prospects**
**MST (millions of short tons)**

|  | 1968 | | 1975 | | 1980 | | 1990 | |
|---|---|---|---|---|---|---|---|---|
|  | percent | MST | percent | MST | percent | MST | percent | MST |
| New Hampshire | 5.7 | 1.79 | 5.6 | 1.92 | 5.4 | 2.05 | 5.1 | 2.3 |
| Maine | 9.6 | 2.94 | 9.5 | 3.26 | 9.3 | 3.46 | 9.0 | 4.06 |
| Massachusetts | 52.2 | 16.52 | 53.1 | 18.2 | 53.9 | 20.4 | 55.2 | 25.0 |
| Greater Boston | 41.1 | 13.21 | 42.1 | 14.4 | 42.4 | 15.8 | 42.7 | 19.2 |
| Vermont | 3.6 | 1.13 | 3.2 | 1.23 | 3.0 | 1.25 | 2.8 | 1.27 |
| Rhode Island | 6.9 | 2.17 | 6.7 | 2.28 | 6.6 | 2.46 | 6.4 | 2.9 |
| Connecticut | 22.0 | 6.95 | 21.8 | 7.42 | 21.7 | 8.07 | 21.4 | 9.5 |

*Source:* Abt Associates, Inc., *The Boston Seaport, 1970-1990*, Cambridge, 1970, p. 42.

About 60 percent of this total use the numerous facilities of the three local giants, White Fuel (Texaco), Exxon, and Northeast Petroleum (independent). Infrequent deliveries to such an excess of uncoordinated facilities have made capital investments for improvements unattractive. All of the terminals are old, lack room for expansion, and will probably be obsolete within ten years. Though most are fairly well maintained, they generally lack adequate safety and oil pollution prevention and abatement equipment. This latter deficiency, however, will probably soon be remedied by the implementation of the Federal Water Pollution Control Act Amendments of 1972. These new oil pollution prevention regulations will impose stringent equipment and operational requirements on terminal operators and provide stiff penalties for violations. If the Coast Guard and the state Department of Natural Resources are provided with adequate funding and manpower to effectively administer and enforce these regulations, private owners will have no choice but to improve conditions around the troublesome tanker/terminal interfaces.

While the distribution and storage capacity of existing private facilities approximates 13 million barrels and is sufficient at present, it might not be able to accommodate any significant increase in petroleum traffic after 1975.[26] Despite this discouraging forecast, the large, vertically integrated controlling corporations appear satisfied with the current situation and do not at present need or want public port services. Moreover, not all consequences of private enterprise can be so directly addressed by legislative actions as those that generate environmental degradation. Outside of undertaking quasi-public ventures in petroleum reception and distribution, there is little external influence that can be exerted on the private oil companies to expand, modernize, or coordinate existing facilities. Private incentive remains on its own to anticipate and respond to any changes in future patterns of supply and demand. Controversies surrounding the fuel shortages of 1973–1974 bear witness that this is not always a flawless mechanism servicing the public welfare.

The character of the tanker fleet currently servicing Boston is as discouraging and seemingly intractable as that of the reception facilities. Boston's terminals were developed to handle the standard workhorse World-War-II vintage T-2 tanker of about 16,000 deadweight tons (dwt). Most other U.S. North Atlantic ports did likewise and for years their channel depth limitations were no great liability. Today, however, Boston finds itself incapable of servicing the new generation of larger petroleum carriers and dependent upon a fleet of small, outdated vessels. Until recently, there has been no compelling incentive for Boston to reassess its receiving capabilities and realign them with the new developments in tanker transport. Since government construction subsidies have not been offered for tankers in the past, most oil companies have been reluctant to build new U.S. flag tankers in American shipyards at two to three times the cost of construction in foreign yards. This disincentive has consequently perpetuated, especially on the coastal runs, a reliance on obsolete product tankers. Furthermore, since Boston's supply sources in the Gulf and the Philadelphia complex have similar depth limitations and are required by the Jones Act to transship refined products in U.S.-built flag vessels, they have experienced little logistical difficulty in sending compatible vessels to Boston. Even the foreign trade, with newer and larger vessels at its disposal, has accommodated itself to Boston's antiquated facilities by utilizing older and smaller tankers. So the Port has continued, without undue hardship, to rely on inner-harbor terminals shackled to approach channels unable to float larger tankers of upwards of 35,000 dwt with drafts of over 40 feet (See Table 3–5.)

The complexion of Boston's present tanker traffic reflects the unfortunate size limitation imposed by its unfavorable terminal sites. In 1969, approximately 660 tankers called at the Port with the average sizes shown in Table 3–6.

This same composition holds true today, for the physical constraints determining it are immutable. Boston's fleet continues to consist primarily of converted World-War-II and early-1950s tankers, 80 percent of which are over twenty-years old.[27] By 1980, these ships should all be scrapped and it is doubtful that they will be replaced by uneconomic, small tankers in the 15,000 to 35,000 dwt range given the low comparative cost of terminals versus tankers. Thus, Boston finds itself in a dilemma; presently restricted for the optimum operation of modern tanker traffic, it must somehow accommodate these larger tankers if it is to remain a major petroleum port.

In marked contrast to Boston's situation has been the trend in world tanker shipping toward increasingly larger ships. It began in the 1950s when prosperity

**Table 3-5**
**Tanker Size and Draft**

| Deadweight (thousand tons) | Length overall (feet) | Maximum draft (feet) |
|---|---|---|
| 300 | 1140 | 80 |
| 250 | 1100 | 62 |
| 100 | 940 | 50 |
| 65 | 820 | 42 |
| 32 | 660 | 34 |
| 27 | 630 | 32 |
| 20 | 565 | 30 |
| 17 | 525 | 30 |

*Source:* Frederic R. Harris, Inc. *Feasibility Investigation: Massport Out-To-Sea Oil Terminal Study, Interim Report,* Boston, 1970, p. 25.

**Table 3-6**
**Average Tanker Deadweights, Boston, 1969**

| Tanker | Deadweight (dwt) |
|---|---|
| American | 25,000 |
| Foreign | 34,000 |
| Total | 29,000 |

*Source:* Frederic R. Harris, Inc., *Feasibility Investigation Massport Out-To-Sea Oil Terminal System, Interim Report,* Boston, 1970, p. 25.

in western Europe and Japan's postwar industrial recovery brought about an enormous and rapid growth of demand for petroleum. In Europe alone from 1957 to 1967, gasoline consumption tripled and consumption of home heating oil and industrial fuel almost quadrupled. Industrialized countries confronted the irony of having to bring oil long distances from its origin. As this thirst for petroleum increased, it became the economic impetus behind the steady growth in tanker size. The closing of the Suez Canal in 1956 added 5000 miles to the voyage from the Middle East to Europe and hastened this growth process. This trend has accelerated in recent years with further proliferation of the automobile, continued industrialization, and expanding residential demands, especially in western Europe, the U.S., and Japan. The energy crisis seems to have made consumption more self-conscious, but it is still uncertain if any significant and permanent long-term abatement can be achieved.

The intense construction of supertankers during this period had been predicated on their ability to transport large volumes of crude oil cheaply over long distances. The economies of size intrinsic in these larger crude carriers are irresistible. Since bulk weight does not increase proportionately with cargo capacity, the construction cost per deadweight ton for a 50,000 dwt tanker is about twice that for a 500,000 dwt tanker; thus, a fleet of ten 50,000 dwt ships would cost nearly twice what one equal capacity 500,000 dwt vessel would cost. Furthermore, the cost per deadweight ton also decreases for manning requirements, auxiliary equipment, maintenance, power requirements, and bunker fuel. In consequence of these factors, the bigger the tanker, the cheaper it is to transport a barrel of oil.

In response to this economic maxim, the world tanker fleet has undergone rapid changes. It has been occupying an increasingly larger proportion of the world's total merchant fleet, and the size of its individual components has swelled incredibly. Total tonnage of the tanker fleet is forecast to increase by 4.7 percent annually until 1990, with large vessels dominating more and more. In 1971, there were 167 tankers of 200,000 dwt or over in operation.[28] For 1975, it was predicted that 47 percent of the total tanker tonnage would be in vessels of 115,000 dwt and over; for 1980, the estimate is 64 percent; and, for 1990, it is 76 percent. At present, 533 tankers in this category are under construction around the world.[29] In March 1973, Britain's Globetik Tankers signed a letter of intent with a Japanese shipyard for a 706,000 dwt tanker — the largest so far in the world. Evaluation and preliminary designs have been completed for a 1,000,000 dwt vessel. It strains the imagination to compare these behemoths with Columbus's 60 dwt *Nina* and the later 180 dwt *Mayflower*. This dramatic and rapid evolution from supertankers to Very Large Crude Carriers (VLCCs) to Ultra Large Crude Carriers (ULCCs) has made the designation of being the "world's largest tanker" a very short-lived distinction.

Since depth limitations in most world ports preclude their accommodation of these larger vessels, there has necessarily been a corollary trend towards deep-water offshore oil terminals for both crude and product carriers. Since 1958, approximately 100 off-shore monobuoy terminal systems have been installed around the world. Some are capable of handling tankers of any size even in severe weather conditions. There are about 60 foreign deep-water port facilities in operation, under construction, or planned which can service 200,000 dwt vessels.[30] A consolidation process is also underway in which a single transshipment terminal will serve an entire region. This more developed stage seems well advanced in the Bantry Bay, Ireland–western Europe distribution system.

These international trends have had a profound impact on the U.S. petroleum scene. Even without a modernized, expanded U.S. tanker fleet, domestic ports will soon be unable to handle the increasingly larger foreign tankers.

Predictably, New England is especially overdue for a more advanced distribution system. In 1970, a study was done to assess possible development plans for oil processing and distribution in New England.[31] It found the region's present system to be in the least developed phase: a large and growing number of small terminals serving associated demand centers. A more developed phase would utilize the economies of scale of transshipment by consolidation of several individual terminals into larger transshipment terminals — such as Portland and Boston — to serve subregions. The most mature phase would be total consolidation in which the entire region would be served by a single transshipment terminal. The study found New England approximately at the stage in which final consolidation of its oil distribution system should take place. A transshipment center in either Eastport or Searsport, Maine — two of the few places on the East Coast where drafts of seventy feet can be accommodated in sheltered waters — was found unfeasible without a companion refinery. The remoteness of both from the principal consumption centers would make for prohibitive distribution costs. Furthermore, later observers have also felt that even a terminal-refinery complex in either Maine or New Hampshire, as proposed by Aristotle Onassis, would initially only service northern New England, with none of the subsequent benefits of an economic and reliable petroleum supply accruing to the eastern Massachusetts population center.

An alternative offshore terminal in the Boston area, however, corresponds to a minimum distribution cost configuration. Since transshipment from any terminal location would be by product tankers and seagoing barges rather than an inflexible pipeline system, Boston's proximity to the center of consumption would allow it the least ton-miles to be distributed. Massachusetts would thus realize a reliable oil supply with substantial savings on fuel costs. The construction of a refinery would further enhance these advantages. Besides bare necessity then, there would be other beneficial reasons to circumvent the limitations of Boston's existing terminal facilities.

In light of these promising alternatives to counter the ominous threat that world shipping trends posed to Boston, Massport, in its own inscrutable manner, came to rescue the Port from its impending downfall as a major petroleum distribution center. Foreseeing both the future difficulties and opportunities for the Port, it commissioned a feasibility study for an offshore oil terminal system that was completed in 1970.[32] At the outset, the study by Frederic R. Harris, Inc. justified Massport's role as the first nonindustry source in the U.S. to sponsor deep-water port development. The report was confident of the practicality and propriety of such an initiative and stated that

... The Massachusetts Port Authority, marine and politically oriented, is considered a practical vehicle to meld and bridge the chasm between the real needs of the people and industry. The Massachusetts Port Authority is indeed in this instance 'catalyst between Commerce and Industry.'[33]

It further believed Massport

> ... would be fulfilling the covenant for which it was established; that is for the benefit of the people of Massachusetts.[34]

Based on this complimentary rationale for Massport action, the study assessed the projected growth of demand against Boston's physical limitations and also evaluated the area as to the feasibility of a local refinery. It found a refinery appropriate since 25 percent of the local market would support a 100,000 bbl/day minimum size refinery. (It took 25 percent of a market as the maximum that can realistically be assigned to any one company in the intensely competitive oil business.) Its final recommendations were for a marine-industrial complex focused around two offshore terminals, a pipeline and tank farm system, and a refinery. The study proposed a two-phase, multiple-user development scheme. The first step would be the construction of a products facility three miles out to sea in water deep enough (mean low water of 55 feet) to accommodate the largest estimated product vessels (70,000–80,000 dwt). The two-berth island pier would use an expandable pipeline system to pump the oil to storage tanks leased by the oil companies or directly to existing terminals. The study saw this project as economically feasible as Massport's construction cost would be approximately $34 million. The total average annual costs (debt service, maintenance, operations) were estimated at $5.99 million. By the fifth year of operation, the annual revenues of $6.05 million would be greater than the annual cost. By about the tenth year, the deficit would be paid off, and the system would provide a source of income for other improvements.[35]

The second stage was to construct an offshore crude oil receiving facility capable of handling tankers in the 300,000 dwt class and above. The proposed two-berth floating pier would be located six miles offshore in 100 feet of water. The cost, estimated between $17 and $23 million, would be shared by several oil companies and paid for by user charges. Simultaneously, a private company would build a $100 to $150 million, 100,000 bbl/day refinery. There were adequate sites off Massachusetts' North Shore for both terminals, and land was available on Belle Isle for the tank farm and in the Lynn Marshes for the refinery. Completing the complex would be the secondary process industries and the tertiary consumer-oriented industries attracted to the area by the availability of raw petroleum materials from the refinery.

The potential benefits from this proposal were tantalizing. The direct delivery of cheap foreign crude, the economics of large tankers, the lower distribution costs with a local refinery, and the increased competition among oil companies could save the area as much as $10 million by 1975 in reduced fuel costs.[36] Direct employment in the refinery and petrochemical industries could mean 3000 new jobs with the potential for another 7500 jobs in spinoff industries. Not only would Massport have another source of revenue, but the local property tax rolls could be increased by several million dollars. On top of every-things else, the entire development would cost the taxpayers absolutely nothing. The inherent value of a more reliable supply of fuel, however, was not yet fully appreciated during these carefree, pre-"Energy Crisis" days.

Massport had seemed to come up with another proposal in which all con-cerned won. Its reception, however, was less than enthusiastic to say the least. The Authority's first mistake was to keep the report a secret for two years, a decision compatible with its penchant for autonomous and exclusive actions, but of no relief to its sagging public relations image or the region's precarious energy future. The firm that prepared the study had obviously been well instructed, for it dutifully, but without further explanation, reported in its Letter of Transmit-tal,

...We have proceeded cautiously with the minimum of local contacts...the total involvement of the Port Authority in the Political, Social and Economic environment of the Greater Boston and New England Regional Community re-quires such a course.[37]

With the report made public, all Massport's Executive Director could offer critics as a justification for the delay was that, "there was no need to alarm anyone."[38]

The general public was indifferent to the disclosure, except for East Boston which had long suffered with the nefarious and omnivorous Logan Airport for a neighbor and was more than slightly paranoid about Massport. These residents saw it as the usual plot to impose another Port Authority project upon the de-fenseless citizenry, despite Massport's insistence that there were five local com-munities that had expressed interest in the refinery. The proposal was opposed by many elected officials, especially state Senator William Bulger, the ecology-minded chairman of the powerful Special Legislative Committee on Marine Boundaries and Resources. He did not mince words, branding the proposal

... an ambitious plan replete with its own sets of contradictions, non sequitors and rationalizations so steeped in its own self-interest that it failed to consider ... factors such as national and regional economic and energy policies.[39]

Governor Francis Sargent, a long-time conservationist and no fan of Massport, simply ignored the study.

So the grandiose proposal never really got off the ground and was put aside to await a more receptive atmosphere. Before long, this new climate was assured by the momentous reorientation of the world petroleum industry that was sud-dently effected by the Arab oil producing states following the October War in the Middle East in 1973. The first manifestation of this new petroregime was an energy crisis that Massport so opportunely forecast in 1969 and which was to revive the concept of an offshore terminal for Boston. International politics had accomplished what local initiative could not. Henceforth, Boston's role as a major petroleum port will have to be more closely integrated with the national conditions and policies that develop in response to a now much more insecure and unpredictable international supply situation.

The ominous ramifications of such an unstable energy future for the U.S. have prompted comprehensive conservation efforts, increased exploration for new domestic sources, and intensified research for alternative sources. With no major breakthrough in sight, national energy self-sufficiency is highly improbable in the foreseeable future. The general consensus seems to be that, to meet growing demands, the U.S. will have to significantly increase foreign oil imports. Some estimates set imports at 7.5 million barrels a day in 1975, 9.3 million in 1980, and 11.6 million in 1985, 65 percent of the total U.S. supply.[40] As the Caribbean basin dries up, U.S. imports will come more and more from North Africa and the Middle East, not withstanding current political difficulties, and necessitate roundtrip voyages of 8,400 and 24,000 nautical miles respectively, for tankers too large to use the reopened Suez Canal. Since, at present, U.S. flag tankers carry only 5 percent of the total national oil imports, the U.S. is ill-prepared to provide transportation for the anticipated increases in foreign oil imports. Consequently it has had to embark on a crash construction program in order to assure that these expanded volumes will be carried in U.S. flag supertankers. Some experts predict that, by 1985, it will require one hundred and twelve 80,000 dwt tankers and two hundred eighty four 250,000 dwt tankers to transport all foreign oil imports in U.S. flag vessels.[41] The benfits of developing this capacity to meet current and projected energy needs until at least 1980 are obvious. Not only would the supply flow be more assured with an independent, modern American tanker fleet, but the use of economical VLCCs and large product tankers would result in significant savings. On the Persian Gulf to Atlantic Coast run, not using the Suez Canal, the per barrel transport costs are $0.89 for a 50,000 dwt tanker and $0.40 for a tanker of 200,000 dwt.[42] In 1985, the cost savings to the U.S. would be approximately $6 million per day or almost $2 billion per year. Other advantages of such a program would be an improved balance of trade, strengthened national security in times of emergency, the supplemental benefits of increased shipyard employment, and a general boost to the economy. Furthermore as the profit margins of the private oil companies are narrowed by the demands of the producing states, increased significance will be placed on minimizing transport costs.

This new approach to the U.S. tanker fleet was indicated earlier in the Merchant Marine Act of 1970. In that year, the U.S. had 301 tankers totaling 7,835,000 dwt compared to a world fleet of 4,144 tankers totaling 142,652,000 dwt.[43] Enabling legislation, sponsored by the Nixon administration with overwhelming bipartisan endorsement, launched the U.S. on a new maritime program. While the general purpose was the private construction of a modern, balanced fleet that would meet the country's needs in both peace and war, it was significant that, for the first time, tankers were to qualify for federal subsidies.

This new policy was soon implemented by the Federal Maritime Administration (MarAd) through its programs of Construction Differential Subsidy and Operating Differential Subsidy. Though at first it was difficult to attract the necessarily large capital investments for tanker construction, before long the lure of Federal funding kindled interest in a national supertanker fleet. MarAd soon recognized that vessel operators were convinced that the economies inherent in the use of VLCCs would dictate their use in all possible trades. Investors felt that building large numbers of "handy" (35,000 dwt) and "intermediate" (85,000 dwt) tankers would economically penalize them by restricting oil imports to smaller vessels. Despite any contrary advantages of flexibility of operation and schedule, especially in the coastal trade, MarAd's policy is one of accommodation rather than direction:

The construction subsidy program is structurally designed to be responsive to the private interests who will own and operate the vessels and invest 60 to 65 percent of the vessel's cost in their own capital. Since operators always have the option of building and registering their ships abroad, the government's influence over the number and types of ships they build with construction subsidy is constrained.[44]

The increasing commitment to VLCCs is indicated in recent construction statistics. Only three tankers were built in U.S. shipyards in 1973, but one was 225,000 dwt and another 190,385 dwt.[45] Of the tankers under contract for construction, eight are greater than 200,000 dwt and sixteen are in the 90,000 dwt class.[46] Construction applications for sixty-five additional tankers are pending before the Maritime Subsidy Board; of these, forty-two are greater than 200,000 dwt, seventeen are within the 80,000 dwt class, and only six are less than 40,000 dwt.[47] This emphasis on larger tankers is likely to increase even further if the pending Energy Transportation Security Act requiring 30 percent of oil imports to be carried by U.S. flag vessels by 1977 is passed by Congress. A similar bill requiring a 50 percent carriage was defeated in the Senate last year, however, and the present bill faces stiff opposition.

As the trend toward VLCCs intensifies, there is increasing pressure to construct offshore terminals to accommodate them. Most existing U.S. ports are limited to 50,000 dwt tankers and a few are able to handle the 90,000 dwt class. Since no U.S. port at present can handle VLCCs above 200,000 dwt (See Table 3-5), offshore facilities are a necessity if the U.S. is to satisfy future demands with huge quantities of foreign oil while realizing the economy of large tankers. Since private investors are determined to utilize VLCCs to the greatest possible extent, the U.S. in effect has no choice but to receive them in deep-water terminals.

Currently, there are about a dozen offshore oil facilities in the U.S., virtually all of them on the West Coast. Generally they are of the monobuoy type in depths of 50 to 60 feet of water. More terminals in deeper water, especially along the other U.S. coasts, are imperative. Some experts, however, feel that such facilities will not be located in the Gulf of Mexico until well after 1975 and on the East Coast only after 1980.[48] Even before the fuel shortage, the urgency of the situation was expressed by President Nixon:

Given these considerations, I believe we must move forward in an ambitious pro-gram to create new deep-water ports for receiving petroleum imports.[49]

This conviction is shared by MarAd in its Environmental Impact Statement for its Tanker Construction Program that also considers the impact of offshore facil-ities, which it views as inevitable adjuncts to VLCC utilization. It concludes that the primary pressure for the construction of such facilities

... comes from both industry and government sources interested in the very sizeable economic savings involved.[50]

It predicts that the development of these terminals will alter the historic port, terminal, and petroleum distribution patterns in the U.S. This national commit-ment to deep-water terminals has resulted in the Deepwater Port Act, which passed Congress after initial difficulties over the choice of a lead agency. The bill basically provides for the licensing of construction and operation of offshore terminals and the establishment of rules and regulations. Conceding that foreign oil imports will constitute a substantial part of U.S. energy sources until at least the end of the century, the House Committee on Merchant Marine and Fisheries, in its report on the bill, stated that

Based upon the economic and environmental considerations involved, the Com-mittee believes that the need for offshore oil ports is clearly demonstrated . . . there is, therefore, need for the creation of a license system related to high seas oil ports if the nation is to be able to take advantage of this transportation system.[51]

The only stumbling block on the road to unbridled enthusiasm for the VLCC-offshore terminal system has been the key issue of environmental protec-tion. This has been especially true in Massachusetts. The original Harris study for Massport identified environmental opposition as a "psychological barrier" that especially afflicted New Englanders who prized their scenic and recreational re-sources, fought against offshore oil drilling on Georges Bank, pursued quixotic law suits such as U.S. vs. Maine, and rejected refineries offered by benevolent foreign capitalists. An increased concentration of public attention on environ-mental problems and oil spills since the first report led Harris to feel it necessary to prepare a supplemental report one year later on the potential environmental impact of its proposed offshore terminal complex. It put forth the usual conten-tion that such a project would not interfere with the adjacent community environment and that there would be minimum detrimental effect on the onshore and offshore ecology. The heart of the argument, which has now become standard for deep-water terminal proponents, was that one could actually expect

... a reduction in oil pollution from oil delivered to a single, ultra-modern terminal designed under the strictest environmental safeguards to accommodate larger shipments from deep draft tankers, as opposed to the present arrangement of delivering oil in smaller ships to two dozen older terminals.[52]

A high-quality terminal, concentrating all the oil companies' efforts and operated by Massport would not only reduce the chance of an oil spill, but, located offshore with better equipment and trained personnel, it would permit a faster and more efficient containment and collection of any oil if there were a spill. Radically fewer tankers would, of course, reduce the occasions for oil spillage. Massport later projected the decrease in traffic in 1985 to be from 1140 35,000 dwt tankers without an offshore terminal to 252 35,000 dwt tankers and 114 300,000 dwt tankers with a terminal.[53]

The environmental conclusions reached by the Harris Report and Massport are not isolated. They have been substantiated through extensive studies by the Intergovernmental Maritime Consultative Organization (IMCO); the Coast Guard; MarAd; the Army Corps of Engineers; the Council on Environmental Quality; the University of Maryland; and prestigious consultants such as Soros Associates, Inc., Robert Nathan Associates, Inc., and Arthur D. Little, Inc. All of these major studies have shown that the risk factor for oil pollution is much less with utilization of VLCCs and offshore terminals than with the present arrangement of older, smaller tankers and inner-harbor terminals. In the fine print, however, most of them admit not considering a VLCC catastrophic spill, a consideration which would "seriously alter" their results. MarAd went so far as to say that

... the chances of all these circumstances being exactly right for maximum damage and resulting irreversible consequences are in the staff's opinion, remote.[54]

The basic reasoning behind this supertanker optimism is appleaing. Even the Chairman of the Council on Environmental Quality was led to comment that

In sum, then, the United States is going to need increasing amounts of imported oil. This oil will be imported in small ships — at greater risk of oil spills — if deep water ports are not available to serve supertankers.[55]

It has been estimated that oil transport accounts for about 1457 million metric tons or 30 percent of the total 4897 million metric tons of annual oil pollution in the oceans. This contribution is made through either casualty discharges or operational discharges. Of casualty discharges, structural failures, groundings, and collisions account for over 86 percent of the total outflow and, with the exception of structural failures, occur predominantly in the coastal waters, harbors and entranceways, and at piers. VLCCs and offshore terminals would dramatically reduce these occurrences in several ways. Since transfers would take place in deep offshore waters, groundings would be practically eliminated. The use of a few large ships would also greatly reduce the collisions presently unavoidable in congested, narrow inner-harbor channels. Furthermore, a spill at an offshore terminal would be less damaging than one in an ecologically fragile coastal marine area. The usual conclusion reached after assessing these advantages is that the potential oil spill factor generally decreases as a function of size, and that it is therefore environmentally safer to transport petroleum by supertankers using off-shore ports than it is by smaller tankers using conventional facilities.[56]

Operational discharges are even more important than casualties, however, since they account for about 82 percent of total oil outfall from oil transport, with the following breakdown: tank cleaning, 70 percent; ballast and other discharges, 7 percent; and terminal transfers, 5 percent. But operational, as well as casualty discharges in the VLCC-offshore terminal system, can be minimized by design, construction, equipment, and operational standards and by rules and regulations incorporating the latest technological advances for safety and pollution prevention, abatement, and cleanup. Applicable safeguards that would hopefully minimize pollution from the extensive use of U.S. supertankers and domestic offshore facilities have been established by a plethora of laws and are implemented by a variety of Federal agencies. These include: Environmental Protection Agency regulations; the Coast Guard Rules and Regulations on Pollution Prevention, Vessel and Oil Transfer Facilities; the Port and Waterways Safety Act of 1972; the MarAd Standard Specifications for Merchant Ship Construction; and the Deepwater Port Act. MarAd's more rigid standards under Section 70 on Pollution Abatement Systems and Equipment are tactfully urged but not required because of the present policy of avoiding affecting a vessel's economic viability in foreign trade. Theoretically, if all these controls were to work to full effect, most of the environmental benefits cited by advocates of supertankers and offshore ports would probably be reasonably assured.

The alternatives to such an appealing arrangement appear, in the long run, neither economically nor environmentally attractive for the nation, New England, or Boston. Retention of the present system would not lower the cost of oil transportation and greater use of Canadian and Caribbean deep-water ports, even if possible, would only increase transshipment in smaller tankers and consequently pollution. Dredging is expensive, ecologically dangerous, and would still limit a port to 80,000 dwt ships; it presents a dredge-spoil disposal problem and again would only increase traffic and oil pollution. Furthermore, there has been mounting opposition from both Maine and Canada to locating a deep-water facility in Eastport, hitherto the most probable site, because of the ecological perils to the pristine northern coastline that the concomitant traffic of mammoth tankers would entail. One of the few pilots now licensed to guide large ships into Eastport, Captain Amos Mills, testified against any such proposals at public environmental hearings, stating that, despite deep water, the fog and currents at Eastport make it an inappropriate site for tanker traffic.[57] So in the end, it has begun to appear that the only way out of their respective dilemmas for both the nation and Boston may be the rising tide of VLCCs and offshore terminals. More people are starting to share the perplexity of a leading industry spokesman:

I am astonished that we are still talking and doing little for the off-shore systems we will require, that we are allowing a few objectors to delay action on something that is so important to the nation.[58]

But action was delayed in Boston, and by more than a few objectors. As indicated above, prior to the local impact of the 1973–1974 Arab oil embargo, environmental sensibilities were affronted enough to prevent any further progress in planning for an offshore terminal complex. Lacking any wide support, the political leadership at Massport muffled their dire predictions and abstained from any visible advocacy of the plans. Massachusetts confronted supertankers and refineries with the same cautious opposition that is generally accorded nuclear power plants. Popular opinion seemed to be that the threat of traumatic oil spills along New England's invaluable coastline was real enough to outweigh the supply and economic portents that lacked the immediacy to arouse a reordering of traditional priorities. Supertankers, in truth, have not had a sterling track record and there seemed sufficient reports of unsettling pollution disasters to justify barring, or at least postponing their arrival in Boston. Offshore oil ports are an even newer factor with even less empirical evidence to attest to their environmental innocence. Even the most dispassionate Massachusetts citizens were convinced, with probable justification, that the issue demanded much further study and better guarantees of environmental protection before warranting any form of commitment. The time was obviously not ripe for introducing a radically new approach to petroleum distribution in the Port of Boston.

Besides the environmental reasons to brake any headlong rush towards an offshore terminal, the supply situation in Boston is not in such dire straits as once feared; this also qualified the urgency, and to an extent the necessity, for a deep-water facility. It had been generally assumed that, once Boston's fleet of small, old tankers was retired, it would be necessary to turn to larger tankers since few of the uneconomical smaller tankers were still being built and operated. This would of course end the usefulness of the Port's physically constrained inner-harbor terminals since they could not accommodate these larger vessels. This scenario is proving somewhat inaccurate as the growing traffic in oceangoing petroleum barges sustains Boston's supply flow through the existing, shallow-draft reception facilities. This increased use of large oceangoing tug and barge units reflects a national trend. Currently, there are more than 1.2 million dead-weight tons of barges with capacities of over 10,000 tons each, the largest of which is a 33,000 ton tank barge.[59] These units are especially efficient and economical because the tug can be separated upon arrival to undertake a new tow while the barge is being serviced, they drastically reduce crew costs, and they are much cheaper to construct than tankers. Moreover, their shallow drafts allow them to maneuver waters that are not deep enough for present-day tankers.

Such units are well suited for Boston, where tanker traffic is steadily declining while barge traffic is steadily rising, reaching a high of 2473 arrivals in 1973, basically all of which were petroleum carriers supplying about 35 percent of the Port's total petroleum volume. The two largest barges servicing Boston, the *Ocean 250* and the *Ingram 3731*, rival the carrying capacity of the traditional modified T-2 Tanker. Tankers will continue to be used at terminals abutting deeper water, while barges will replace them at the more restrictive sites, especially along the Chelsea Creek. These new barges may also prove to be less of a pollution hazard than Boston's current aged tanker fleet because of their shallower drafts and improved design and construction. These "superbarges" are demonstrating that Boston's petroleum situation is more flexible than generally believed and that its supply prognosis need not be as desperate as often pictured. Reliance on barges will not, however, completely deflate the rationale for an offshore port, although some people feel that the further development of the present system could negate any need for a crude oil terminal and refinery complex if other sources of refined products could be assured. It remains, however, that there would undoubtedly be considerable economic savings and distribution advantages with a product terminal and regional pipeline.

Despite these valid uncertainties about the wisdom, timing, or extent of offshore port development for Boston, international petroleum politics soon introduced new considerations that unsettled local attitudes. During the notorious energy disruptions of 1973-1974, the climate in Boston seemed to mellow to such a proposal, and the initial indifference and hostility of the fall of 1972 were considerably dissipated. The "psychological barriers" cited by the first Harris report were noticeably weakened by the well-extolled economic and environmental virtues of a VLCC-offshore terminal system and, even more so, by the inconvenience of long gas lines and the discomfort of lowered thermostats. In late 1973, Massport called for a final $500,000 indepth study by the consulting engineers at Harris. Shortly thereafter, Massport's Executive Director termed an offshore terminal "more important than ever now that the nation is in the throes of an energy crisis."[60] He found unexpected supporters. The Massachusetts Congressional delegation telegramed their endorsement, calling the plan "timely, innovative and deserving of further complete study."[61] Even the Governor's Secretaries of Transportation and Environmental Affairs now approved it as a "worthwhile venture."[62] Eventually, even the unregenerate Chairman of the Special Legislative Committee on Marine Resources and Boundaries made a proposal strikingly similar to Massport's except, viewing Massport's state plan as inefficient and uneconomic, he, along with the Governor's most recent appointee to the Port Authority's board, favored a more regional approach.[63]

In the end, however, it was Governor Sargent, overcoming his original indifference, who best evidenced the changing times. In December 1973, while his own Energy Emergency Program was being cut to pieces by a special session of the legislature, he issued a "major policy statement on oil refineries" to assure that Massachusetts was not left out of the planning for terminal complexes then going on for Sanford and Eastport, Maine and Durham, New Hampshire. His proposal called for: (1) one or two deep-water terminals owned and regulated by a public agency which would receive all the crude oil for New England, (2) a regionally owned or regulated pipeline system, (3) environmentally designed inland refineries, and (4) a public voice in the kinds of petroleum products to be produced.[64] Since, with a few embellishments, his plan was curiously similar to the Harris· recommendations, the Governor, to his credit, said his proposal was based in large part on what Massport had originally suggested.

So now, with bipartisan encouragement, a more extensive and indepth study was conducted to concentrate solely on the feasibility of a system, as outlined in the initial Harris report, to receive, refine, and distribute crude oil. Massport seemed to have decided that it was preferable to pursue maximum development to allow for direct foreign crude import rather than a less ambitious and possibly less controversial product terminal. The final report was done in three separate components — economic, environmental, and engineering — and its overall findings supported the preliminary 1969 study. It concluded that local crude oil receipt and refining would have significant economic benefits, increase employment, improve the tax base, and have an acceptable environmental impact. A subsequent site selection study incorporated all considerations and, in addition, paid particular attention to the crucial political factor of community acceptance of a terminal, refinery, tank farm, and pipeline. It found a site off Newburyport, north of Boston near the New Hampshire border, to be the most economically viable and environmentally attractive location, with the local citizenry clearly welcoming a deep-water port complex in their region.

All of these studies seem to have laid sufficient groundwork for rational decision making, although many still feel that the environmental consequences are not adequately enough understood to justify acquiescence. The issue transcends purely local concern and any determination and implementation will have to be accomplished at the regional level within the context of national and international conditions. A slight possibility is that, under the 1972 Coastal Zone Management Act, the usual state prerogative for regulating coastal development could be preempted, and the federal government, in "the interest of national security," could override local opposition or indecision and authorize an offshore port program for New England. Whether Boston's traditional technological lag will prove its undoing as the major oil port for New England has yet to be seen. Petroleum traffic has played a critical role in the Port's recent history and could play an even more important role in the future. The outcome, decided by whatever combination of necessity, politics, passion, and externalities, remains uncertain.

# 4

## Constitution of the Port: Port Facilities and Cost Structure

*Functionless property is the greatest enemy of legitimate property itself.*
Richard H. Tawney

**Port Facilities**

In Boston, as with many ports, waterfront facilities can be divided into two broad categories. First there are the privately owned and operated facilities for handling bulk cargoes. While petroleum terminals were discussed earlier, dry bulk traffic, of relatively less importance, will not be treated in any depth. Public general cargo facilities, however, deserve more attention. Although the condition of terminal facilities and cargo handling equipment has rarely been a decisive factor in a shipper's decision to use a port other than Boston, until recently these important components of Boston's image have been a negative influence and a needless financial drain.

Besides its petroleum facilities, Boston has nine other private facilities for bulk commodities; two for scrap metal, two for bulk cement, two for salt, one for gypsum, one for sugar, and one for mixed products. While adequate at present with water depths of about 43 feet, these facilities face imminent problems similar to those of the Port's petroleum terminals. As dry bulk carriers undergo a parallel rapid increase in size, they will greatly exceed the capability of the available bulk-offloading facilities in Boston. This incompatibility will eventually evolve as another unavoidable predicament for the Port.

General cargo facilities, however, are of much more importance to any port. "The capacity and efficiency of the marine terminals represent the major investment of a seaport in providing for present cargo needs and also developing its future potential for an expanded flow of commerce."[1] In light of this, Boston would seem to have certain advantages. Its facilities are generally well maintained and are adequate for the present and foreseeable volume of cargo moving through the Port. It has an excellent natural harbor and is the closest U.S. port to Northern Europe. Its waterfront piers are only 5 to 7 miles from the open ocean, compared to 103 for Philadelphia and 150 for Baltimore. New York is also close to the ocean, within about 20 miles, but Boston offers easier navigation due to less congestion. Boston's three major channels can handle all ships engaged in or planned for general world trade. It has 259 piers or wharves along 158,646 lineal feet (30 miles) of berthing space with about 30 active berths for ships up to 800 feet with drafts of 39 feet. The Port offers more than sufficient related maritime services such as freight forwarders, commercial banking services, consular services, and relevant government agencies, i.e., U.S. Customs, Department of Agriculture, Food and Drug Administration, Immigration and Naturalization Service.

Despite these advantages, except for specialized operations, steamship companies do not lease or own any facilities because of the declining status of the Port and the low tonnage volume it offers. Boston is not alone in this situation. Over the last fifty years, the inability of terminals to operate profitably has resulted, especially in the North Atlantic ports, in facilities being turned over from private to public interests for operation, often with the aid of public funds. This process has given Massport the ownership of all but one of the regularly used general cargo berths in East Boston, Charlestown, and South Boston, which it either operates itself or leases. The irrefutable evidence that recent advances in seaport technology can significantly lower the cost of port operations makes this stewardship all the more critical.

Undermining this apparently acceptable situation is the Port's vast excess of obsolete, inefficient facilities. In 1968, the port director explained that property expansion projects were deferred because Boston was operating at only 6 percent of its potential efficiency. Rather than lacking pier facilities, it was fifteenth among U.S. ports in efficiency.[2] A later study more clearly demonstrated this excess of facilities. It found that, even with regular container service, Boston would average only six ships in port per day through 1990. The probability of more than seven ships in port at any one time was set at less than 5 percent, and the probability of more than nine "would conceivably only occur as a result of strikes or acts of God."[3]

Added to this burden of overabundance is the obsolete condition of most facilities. Before they were permanently shut down in 1966, Boston's last two grain elevators were antiquated and undersized with a combined capacity of less than 2 million bushels. As a result, the loading of a 400,000 bushel cargo, which averaged twelve hours in Baltimore and Norfolk, required twenty-eight hours in Boston.[4] The railroad piers built after World War II were a more serious liability and soon obsolete in a port where trucks serviced 85 percent of the cargo traffic. Terminals designed essentially for rail freight are only adapted with difficulty to truck freight and, therefore, contribute to the high cost of cargo handling.

Land transfers are slow and difficult because of the broad scattering of small facilities, many of which have extremely limited and confined access and are remote from cargo consolidation points and junctions of other transportation systems such as major arteries and feeder lines. Furthermore, the Port has suffered from lack of cargo security, insufficient truck marshalling and apron space, and inadequate pier cargo-handling facilities.

Given these obstacles to development, Massport has been the target of two major lines of criticism. The first of these is that it has ignored port investments while lavishing funds upon Logan Airport. The Boston Shipping Association, with no love lost bewteen it and Massport, was a reliable source of such accusations, complaining that, among other things, "The Massachusetts Port Authority has used twice as much money for improving an airport restaurant as it has allocated for improving all pier properties in the Port."[5] Such charges were well justified until only recently. An example of this was the bond issue Massport floated in 1964, from which $31,088,468 was designated for airport improvements while only $1,040,000 went toward port improvements. By its own reckoning, between 1959 and 1967, Massport invested over $100 million for capital improvements in Logan Airport while less than $10 million went toward the "rehabilitation" of the seaport.[6]

This policy of reconditioning the Port lent itself to the other major criticism: that Massport was improvidently expending funds to repair and maintain an excess of obsolete and inefficient facilities while not initiating any new development projects. Some investments were warranted, such as the million dollar dockside freezer at Commonwealth Pier to stimulate shipments of frozen foods via Boston. Others, however, were disastrous, such as the $448,000 reconstruction of Pier 3 in East Boston to accommodate the Challenger class vessels of the United States Lines, which, shortly thereafter, closed its Boston office. The worst example, however, was the millions of dollars Massport spent rebuilding its rail terminals, for which it was justifiably accused of perpetuating inefficiency. While 58 percent of Boston's port expenditures went for the repair of old facilities, its rival ports on the North Atlantic averaged only 21 percent. While all had begun construction programs averaging $50 million in each port, Boston had not even a plan for such projects. Until the late 1960s, Massport was deservingly rebuked: "The Massachusetts Port Authority is the only agency on the North Atlantic Range which has yet to undertake any significant building program aimed at providing new facilities for the efficient flow of commerce through the port."[7]

In defense of Massport on the first count, its disproportionate investment in Logan Airport and relative negligence of the Port should have been reasonably anticipated given the business ethic upon which the new authority was founded. Because of the nature of its independent revenue bond financial structure, Massport, with the insight of a good merchant, felt it had to be certain that its initial investments were of high quality and promised significant returns in order to develop a commercial reputation that would guarantee it a receptive market for future bond issues.

The critical importance of bondholders and the sensitivity of the bond market generally led Massport to be highly attentive to the interests of its investors while appearing callous toward any consideration of a countervailing public interest. Furthermore, as a later study pointed out, there was a collateral motivation for such a policy: "Statutory provisions requiring port profits to return to the Commonwealth to repay outstanding debts, coupled with the uncertain economic future of the Port, have simply made it unattrative for the Massa-chusetts Port Authority to allocate large resources to the Port's improvement."[8] Because of this complex of encouraging and discouraging factors, all indications for sensible investments pointed to airport runways rather than waterfront piers.

Since Massport receives no external financing as do the public agencies in Philadelphia, Baltimore, and Norfolk, it is dependent entirely on internal re-sources. Initially, it had only the Mystic Bridge for a credit base. Later, however, selective investments added Logan Airport to this secure base and allowed for additional bond issues to fund new and more ambitious capital projects. It all made good, if not unanimously appreciated, business sense. Many attacks on Massport's fiscal behavior as being inconsistent with the public interest and a just ordering of social priorities are self-admittedly valid only as an "extremely broad critique of the inherent nature of independent public authorities and the 'reve-nue bond cycle'."[9] Massport has set out to do what it was intended to do and its approach, so far, has been fairly successful; in its first ten years of existence, it was able to float $204.2 million worth of bonds. Revenues in fiscal 1973 amounted to $24,920,000 from the airport, $5,424,000 from the bridge, and $6,796,000 from the Port.[10] Port expenditures, however, exceeded revenues, as usual, so Massport paid nothing to the Commonwealth. In fact, since it has run small deficits most years, the amount Massport owes the state for the port debt has actually *increased* over the original sum defined in the 1958 Enabling Act. In contrast, both the bridge and the airport have become more profitable ventures, as a direct result, in the case of the airport, of capital improvements. (See Table 4–1.) Not only have Massport's efforts made Logan the world's eighth busiest airport, but it has turned it into a community asset, one of the principal factors in attracting new business to the area.[11]

**Table 4–1**
**Bridge and Airport Use, 1960, 1973**

|  | Fiscal Year 1960 | | Fiscal Year 1973 | |
|  | Logan Airport | Mystic River Bridge | Logan Airport | Tobin Memorial Bridge |
| --- | --- | --- | --- | --- |
|  |  |  |  | (AKA Mystic River Bridge) |
| Total Motor Vehicle Traffic |  | 20,744,116 |  | 25,444,559 |
| Total Domestic and International Traffic |  |  |  |  |
| Flights | 114,070 |  | 250,000 |  |
| Passengers | 2,932,231 |  | 10,757,000 |  |
| Cargo (lbs.) | 57,436,000 |  | 331,766,000 |  |

*Source: Massachusetts Port Authority Annual Reports 1960 and 1973.*

As for the early lack of new port programs and the wasteful maintenance-repair syndrome, Massport was surely remiss. Executive Director Edward King, both for the reasons cited above and because of personal predilection, initiated a policy for immediate airport improvement with no comprehensive development plan for the Port. In fact, there appeared to be little genuine enthusiasm for Boston's future with either grain or break-bulk cargoes. Still, it seems unwise in retrospect to have spent large amounts of money to simply shore up existing facilities and halfheartedly try to keep the Port from falling too far behind its competitors. Eventually, in the late 1960s, attitudes and actions changed with the adoption of a policy of total containerization of the seaport. Though more progress might have been made if Massport had assumed an earlier and more aggressive development program, there seemed to be little sense of urgency until the Authority became convinced that containerization was Boston's first real opportunity to escape its long-time stagnation. Local initiative was aroused when this opportunity seemed threatened by the faster adaptation to the new technology of intermodal transport by Boston's rival North Atlantic ports. Since then, Massport has invested $2 million in a Castle Island container crane, $25 million in the Mystic Container Terminal, and has plans for an additional $40–47 million container terminal. The direction of the Port toward containerization will be discussed more fully in a later chapter.

## Cost Structure

The main reason for evaluating the Port of Boston's cost structure is its significance in the campaign to lure local shippers and consignees, presently using New York, to Boston. Since 85 percent of the exports and 50 percent of the imports of the New England region move through New York, this is no mean task. The actual cost per ton of cargo, as determined by port efficiency, labor productivity, and vessel turnaround time, enters to a varying degree into decisions to reroute. In the North Atlantic zone, the proximity of several major ports makes a transfer of traffic based on cost experience to an alternate port all that much easier. Studies have shown that the lack of frequent steamship schedules, a high pilferage and damage rate, and low labor productivity at Boston constitute the prime rationale behind the diversion of New England traffic through New York. Terminal charges, in this perspective, are not of decisive import, but they nonetheless are taken into consideration by shippers, consignees, and vessels when deciding which port can be most economically patronized.

The most important terminal charges are those for dockage, loading and unloading, usage, wharfage, and demurrage. Dockage is levied against a vessel for the use of berthing space. At 50¢ per ton, Boston's rate is as low or lower than those at the other four major North Atlantic ports. Being a relatively low cost item charged to steamship operators, it has little effect on cargo movements or ship scheduling. Moreover, Boston's method of assessment based on tons of cargo loaded and/or discharged is advantageous to a port handling comparatively low volumes of cargo per vessel. New York's system of assessment based on the gross registered tonnage of a vessel, on the other hand, favors a port where more cargo is handled per sailing.[12] Handling 500 tons of cargo for a vessel of 10,000 gross registered tons would be cheaper in Boston, while handling 1000 tons of cargo for the same vessel would be cheaper in New York.

Loading and unloading charges are for moving cargo from a pier to a rail car or truck and, in some instances, include placing the cargo inside of the rail car or truck. The per ton rate at Massport-operated piers for most unpalletized general cargo is $3.80 for rail cars and $4.00 for trucks; this rate is lower than that of any other North Atlantic port except Hampton Roads. Prior to Massport's control, the charges of independent contractors were the highest of all five major North Atlantic ports.[13] The potential benefits of this cost advantage, however, are not fully realized. While truckers have either absorbed these charges in their line haul rate or passed them on to shippers or consignees, the railroads have always absorbed them. In 1965, however, the New York Central and the Boston & Maine stopped absorbing car loading and unloading charges and began publishing tariffs that covered the cost of this service. Boston is the only major North Atlantic port where rail lines do not absorb these charges on rail line haul traffic. Even in New York, these services, along with lighterage, are absorbed by the railroads and not passed on to the shipper or consignee. The refusal of the Boston rail lines to continue this practice results in the diversion of rail traffic to other ports and the displacement of freight from rail carriers to truck lines.

A usage charge is levied against land carriers, especially truckers, who choose not to use Massport's handling services and perform their own loading or unloading using the equipment and labor of independent companies. At $1.80 per ton, Boston has the highest usage cost of all North Atlantic ports for a seemingly self-defeating purpose. It is believed such charges will act as an incentive to use the new terminal handling services and, thus, give local waterfront labor more work; there is irony in this scheme. While Boston's longshoremen must appreciate this solicitous gesture, it encourages the very situation — i.e., the use of local labor — that justifiably discourages most shippers. There have been increasing complaints about this usage charge, and it has caused some Massachusetts companies to use New York for their shipping needs.

Wharfage is a charge against cargo passing over or onto terminal facilities. Up to 1966, at Massport and all other piers, this was a uniform charge to shipper or consignee based on the tonnage volume of cargo. This proved to be a discriminatory and undesirable practice, however, since terminal operators, still influenced by the original ownership and operation of these facilities by the railroads, didn't assess or collect wharfage charges from the rail lines, while truckers had to bear the full freight cost.[14] With 85 to 90 percent of Boston's traffic handled by trucks, this was a glaring inequity. Massport, with the responsibility to take the initiative in such situations, devised a new approach to shift traditional ways and require full rates for all services performed. In 1966, under a new system, Massport facilities set a charge of $1, later reduced to 70¢ per ton of cargo against the vessel for both rail and truck carriage. Other operators continued to charge $1.75 per ton against shippers and consignees for truck freight but not for rail freight. Boston has been the only port to attempt a more equitable distribution of this charge, a procedure vociferously protested by the Boston Shipping Association (BSA), the local trade agency representing shipping interests.[15] Establishing the highest wharfage charges against vessels of all North Atlantic ports, Massport's new policy ignited an "ungentlemanly and even childish exchange of accusations."[16] It was feared that such a charge when assessed against the water carrier might, depending upon the amount of the charge relative to other port costs and volume of cargo, influence the scheduling of vessels at Boston and possibly lead to the elimination of Boston as a port of call. This has not been the case, however, for since the new arrangement was instituted, general cargo traffic has increased rather than decreased. This was the first vigorous action taken by Massport in the realm of terminal charges, and, in retrospect, it has been both equitable and successful.

The final charge, demurrage, is a penalty assessed for the failure to move cargo from a pier within a given period. In Boston, it is a modest 5¢ per hundredweight per day, but there has been insistent criticism from shippers and consignees that the five-day free-time period for inward cargo, the shortest of all North Atlantic ports, works an unreasonable and costly hardship.

All in all, port terminal charges in Boston have been brought to a reasonable level and do not appreciably weaken, in themselves, the Port's competitive position. Massport has exerted effective leadership in this area and deserves the credit for a viable cost structure at the Port's terminals. It has become obvious, however, that the present tariffs badly need revision due to recent cost increases and inflation; hopefully, a minimum of dissension and defection will accompany whatever adjustments Massport feels are necessary.

# 5

## Constitution of the Port: Labor and Competition with New York

*No strike has ever been lost.*
Eugene V. Debs

### Labor

Labor is a critical factor in any port's development or decline. Its cost and productivity are the major ingredients in a port's total cost structure. Moreover, the quality, consistency, and reliability of waterfront labor can either maintain existing shipping or instigate its transfer to an alternate port and either attract additional traffic or discourage it. Though all North Atlantic ports have experienced labor problems, Boston's troubles have been traditionally inordinate due to certain unique and injurious labor practices. Its reputation in the trade as a high cost "dog port," to be avoided if possible, has persisted and proven difficult to shake.

Boston has had more than its share of labor problems and their impact on the Port has been regrettable. Longshore labor cost is the primary expense associated with cargo operation. As such, it and related costs compose the major consideration in assessing the comparative costs of shipping cargo through the various North Atlantic ports. The use of waterfront labor as a criterion has become even more decisive since the already high and still increasing costs, both direct and indirect, associated with it at all East Coast ports are prompting steamship lines to consolidate traffic at fewer ports, and, if possible, solely at New York. This trend is even more noticeable among container lines.

At first glance, standard labor costs among North Atlantic ports would seem natural, given the existing system of labor contracts. New York is the center of labor-management activity, and the "master contracts" negotiated there are adopted by the local branches of the International Longshoremen's Association (ILA) at all other North Atlantic ports. These agreements involve wages, hours, pension and welfare funds, and contract duration and cover longshoremen, terminal clerks, checkers, tallymen, and watchmen. Local issues are left to be resolved at individual ports, but most are ultimately patterned after similar settlements in New York. It is the great disparity among local labor rules, customs, and practices, however, that gives rise to varying levels of productivity and stevedore and longshoremen costs at each port. As the traditionally bottom rung on this ladder of efficiency, Boston has maintained the lowest labor productivity and, consequently, in most instances, the highest actual labor costs of all East

81

Coast ports. Although more recent figures won't be available until a current study of comparative labor costs is completed, the older figures in Tables 5-1 and 5-2 reflect a situation that prevailed for many years.

**Table 5-1**
**Tons Per Hour Per Draft, Selected Commodity Types**
**(discharge cargo only)**

| Commodity | | Tons per hour | | | |
|---|---|---|---|---|---|
| | Boston | New York | Philadelphia | Baltimore | Hampton Roads |
| General cargo | 13 | 20 | NA* | 26 | 28 |
| Burlap, bales | 26 | 35 | 35 | 38 | 45 |
| Raw wool, Australian, bales | 19 | NA | 26 | NA | 35 |
| Tapioca flour, bags | 16 | 25 | 23 | NA | 36 |
| Lumber | 16 | 29 | 28 | 35 | NA |
| Sugar, bags | 19 | NA | 25 | 42 | 36 |
| Average discharge/ hour | 18.2 | 27.3 | 27.4 | 35.3 | 36 |

*Commodity not discharged at that port or figure not available.
*Source:* Arthur D. Little, Inc., *North Atlantic Port Survey: Report to the Boston Shipping Association,* Cambridge, 1966.

There are other factors, moreover, which have aggravated this situation. General cargo vessels calling on Boston load or unload relatively small average shipments. The tasks of preparing and finishing a ship, when spread over the entire total cargo, result in only a slight increase in expense per ton. When they are required for a small cargo, however, as in Boston, the increase in expense per ton is significant. Boston's traffic also consists of mixed cargoes of many small shipments. This entails time-consuming changes in commodity-handling techniques and reduces productivity. Finally, cargo destined for Boston is stowed differently than New York-bound cargo. The larger New York shipments are usually stowed in the center of a hold where they are quickly and easily reached. Boston's shipments, on the other hand, are stowed in the back or on the sides of a hold, from which unloading requires more time.[1] This situation, incidentally, also affects the Port's export traffic. Since exports loaded at Boston on a vessel bound next for New York would interfere with unloading the remaining inbound cargo, many shipping lines are unwilling to accept the usually small amount of exports available in the Port.

These elements consitute only a minor contribution to Boston's unfavorable labor conditions, however. It has been the high labor costs and low productivity that have created the problems with which the steamship lines cannot profitably

**Table 5-2**
**Stevedore Costs Per Revenue Ton**
(dollars)

| | Average of loading costs 18-month sample survey | | | Average of discharging costs 18-month sample survey | | |
|---|---|---|---|---|---|---|
| | Accessorial costs | Longshore costs | Total | Stevedoring costs | Longshore costs | Total |
| Boston | 9.96 | 6.58 | 16.54 | 7.55 | 5.36 | 13.01 |
| New York | | | | | | |
| North River (old piers) | 12.99 | 5.45 | 18.44 | 12.94 | 5.20 | 18.14 |
| North River (new piers) | 9.52 | 5.05 | 14.57 | 12.50 | 5.46 | 17.96 |
| Brooklyn | 5.77 | 10.01 | 15.78 | NA | NA | NA |
| Philadelphia | 9.74 | 4.26 | 14.00 | 7.97 | 3.48 | 11.45 |
| Baltimore | 6.00 | 3.58 | 9.58 | 3.54 | 3.18 | 6.72 |
| Hampton Roads | | | | | | |
| Newport News | 6.24 | 3.59 | 9.83 | 2.61 | 3.91 | 6.52 |
| Norfolk | 5.21 | 4.14 | 9.35 | 2.32 | 2.85 | 5.17 |

*Source:* Arthur D. Little, Inc., *North Atlantic Port Survey: Report to the Boston Shipping Association,* Cambridge, 1966.

live. Vessels costing up to $10,000 a day to operate can no longer endure being idle due to labor troubles. In 1967 alone, sixty-two ships were lost to Boston and 183 landings canceled due to labor difficulties.[2] As conventional vessels are phased out in favor of container ships, labor inconveniences will be even more intolerable: "Ships will continue to be diverted from Boston because they encounter delays and uncertainties, miss sailing dates and lose business in other ports."[3]

This process of attrition would seem especially relevant to local business lost to New York. Many observers feel that, if Boston's stevedoring costs were equal to or lower than New York's, Boston would soon be sought as a port for all the traffic of its natural hinterland that has customarily used New York. This is not necessarily true, for although Philadelphia, Baltimore, and Hampton Roads have lower per ton labor charges than New York, they all lose much cargo to New York for other reasons. Nevertheless, in the long run, reduced labor costs will aid Boston in its efforts to maintain present ship services, attract new ones, and increase its volume of general cargo freight.

Even without a precise and consistent corollation between labor cost and cargo diversion, a survey of local importers and exporters revealed that three of the four major reasons that they use New York are labor related.[4] Boston has the worst record of pilferage of all U.S. ports, and, since the steamship companies usually pay for these losses, their increased reluctance to call on Boston is easily understandable. Local shippers blame government officials and port management for low labor productivity and efficiency. Finally, careless cargo handling by longshoremen has been both irritating and costly. It has been common for them to use grappling hooks indiscriminately on furniture and damage 20 to 25 percent of a cargo of special paper by using crowbars on the rolls. Such cavalier attitudes are an additional reason why it often appears more sensible to use New York rather than Boston, notwithstanding extra land carrier charges often amounting to $2.38 a hundredweight or $250,000 a year.

Behind this ruinous set of waterfront circumstances lies "a long history of labor difficulties, many of which stem from union efforts to maintain outmoded practices out of a fear of losing wages. Labor conservatism takes the form of overly restrictive work rules and general resistance to technological innovation."[5] The most important of these rules and practices that have historically engendered the underutilization of manpower in the Port of Boston are:

1. Featherbedding — the use of excess personnel, especially clerks.
2. Shape-ups — a procedure by which dock workers are hired and gangs formed at eight o'clock each morning. This usually entails a delay of up to two hours before actual work begins and results in chronic gang shortages.
3. Refusal of longshoremen to work until a full gang is present. In most other ports, regular gangs work short until they are filled through their hiring systems.

4. Practice of leaving work uncompleted on one ship to go to work on another that offers work of longer duration.

5. Limited flexibility in job assignments — gangs can not be shifted from one location or task to another demanding more immediate attention.

6. Lapping — an ingenious system of continuous work breaks that keeps at least two men missing from a gang at all times.

7. Refusal to palletize goods, although prepalletized cargo will be handled. Unnecessary break-bulk results in extra time consumption during loading and unloading.

8. Restricting sling loads to one ton, whereas one-and-one-half to two tons is accepted practice in other ports.

9. The esteemed prerogative of individual members to pick and choose their hours, the amount of work to be done, and what cargoes they would and would not handle. No punitive action is ever taken by the union.

10. Pilferage — highest rate of all U.S. ports. Local longshoremen consider it an established fringe benefit. Security has been lax, especially when a shipment of good scotch whiskey arrives. Further delays result from the customary walkout or work-stoppage when an indignant violator is apprehended.

11. Wildcat strikes — Boston labor has strategically relied on "quickies" of about thirty minutes rather than the general strike which attracts bad publicity. The precipitating issue is usually over the classification of cargo to make possible extra wages. Work-stoppages on loaded piers, given the tight economics of shipping, are usually successful.

With so great a choice of topics to clash over, labor-management relations in Boston have been understandably rocky. In 1946, the Boston Shipping Association (BSA) was established to represent the carriers in negotiations with the ILA. By 1954, a new, rational approach was perceptible on the part of management in contrast to its prior crusty and stubborn pomposity. The BSA was gradually realizing that certain union claims were valid and could be equitably granted. In the end, however, it has not been very much more successful than its predecessors. Traditional labor rules and practices have been grudgingly and superficially modified, but no genuine, permanent, or comprehensive improvements in Boston's labor structure have been attained. Day-to-day operations belie optimistic waterfront rhetoric.

The relations among management, labor, and Massport have not been as amicable as desired. Though its representatives participate in negotiations, Massport would prefer either dealing directly with labor or removing itself completely from the process. It has charged that the weak management of the BSA has allowed the unions to perpetuate outmoded work practices.[6] Concurrently lashing out in the other direction, Massport's Port Director, convinced labor is strangling the Port, bluntly stated that "Labor is featherbedding in every possible way. Union leaders believe they have a God-given obligation to put as many men on a job as possible." To which the New England Vice President of the ILA retorted: "He's a liar. If anything, we do better than anybody. They [management] cry all the way to the bank."[7] Meanwhile, all factions have been roundly criticized on the same controversy by the press: "The fatcat days of the 1950's are over. No longer can the port, the steamship companies or labor afford the luxury of excessive manning tables for gangs working ships."[8]

Two basic issues have hampered cooperative labor-management relations: wages and automation. Wage disputes have been historically founded upon the dilemma of providing reasonable and adequate income to individual laborers while minimizing employer costs. The spiraling cost of living has necessitated periodic consultation and conflict between management and union leaders. With automation, labor's goal of maximum employment is incompatible with management's efforts to reduce costs by utilizing new technological developments. Unilateral attempts to impose capital-intensive operations on dock workers desperately clinging to labor-intensive procedures inevitably increases tension and strife.

Though some settlements have been reached, a "pattern of noncooperativeness" has persisted that appears to have two historical roots. One is the long struggle for existence that longshoremen unions had to endure, breeding a bitterness toward shipping management that still exists. The second source is the conservatism of the shipping industry which, until recently, has allowed archaic traditions on the part of both labor and management to harden as in no other business. Innovations have generally never been well received in the maritime community.

There have also been secondary factors that have abetted poor labor-management relations in Boston. The Port's union is considered "closed," with limited membership cards passed down to members of the family. No other North Atlantic port has such a strict barrier to enrollment. An inadequate number of union members has, in the past, necessitated a high dependence on the time-consuming recruitment of "casual" labor. The average age of union members is 58, with men 50–75 years old predominating. Not only are these men unable to efficiently work a full day, but their years tend to focus their attention on their own short-term interests rather than the future welfare of the Port. Longshoremen in Boston tend to be more independent and undisciplined than most, often not honoring the agreements negotiated by their own representatives and accepted by a vote of all union members. Union leadership, meanwhile, is responsive to its constituents and has protected labor rolls from interference and reduction.

Despite all these obstacles, several formal agreements have been negotiated though they haven't always been observed. In 1954, the first workable grievance procedure was established which, through the conscientious actions of both the BSA and the ILA, has somewhat limited "quickie" strikes. In 1966, the traditional shape-up was abandoned and a central hiring system was adopted. Under this procedure, longshoremen would begin work at a scheduled time because of day-before hiring. Thirty permanent gans of twenty-two men each would commence work at 8:00 A.M. even if short, and a longshoreman would not be allowed to move on to a more favorable ship. Union rolls would be opened and regular gangs with allegiance to a particular stevedore would eliminate "casualization" of the labor force. In exchange for these concessions, longshoremen were guaranteed 1600 hours of pay a year. All port interests were optimistic that this new arrangement would result in steadier work and increased productivity. Soon, however, management claimed that the union was deliberately understaffing gangs, and lack of discipline and confusion among the new gangs actually reduced labor productivity.

In 1969, after more hopeful bargaining and a 104-day strike, a new agreement was reached. It was touted as the first modernization in the Port's labor contracts since 1935. Appearing to insure higher labor productivity, this agreement was taken as proof that Boston was assuming a stability of seaport operations which it had not enjoyed in many years. Both the BSA and ILA were to be congratulated: "With the firm footing of a workable labor contract, they are erasing the myths of the old Boston, and concentrating on bringing as much additional business as possible into the Port of Boston."[9] Behind this optimistic three-year contract was the conviction of John F. "Red" Moran, International Vice President and President of Boston's local ILA. Moran finally decided that the lot of the dock workers could only be improved by a truce with management that would allow the revival of the Port. Thus he conceded not to fight containerization and agreed that his men would work on the same basis as those in New York's container terminal at Port Elizabeth, New Jersey.

The 1969 contract largely lifted work restrictions. It abolished all artificial sling-load requirements, allowed the full utilization of pallets and the handling of containers with the use of ship's gear, reduced the size of gangs, and eliminated the minimum manning requirement. It gave management more latitude in the numbers and uses of clerks and gave it the right to shift gangs from one ship to another or from one hatch to another. Furthermore, it prohibited strikes, walkouts, and lockouts; opened the union register to additional men; and allowed management participation in the hiring hall to insure that all available men were assigned where they were needed the most. In exchange for these improvements and limited cooperation with automation, the ILA's demands were met for 2080 guaranteed hours of work per year at more than twice the previous hourly wage.

Unfortunately, this progressive, comprehensive agreement has been undermined by the continuation of the infamous work habits of Boston's waterfront labor. Gangs of unspecified number report for work late and/or short of men. A gang will still leave a ship, without permission, for another that offers longer work and will often leave a ship before a job is completed. Inevitably, resort to the "quickie" strike has been neither abolished nor even abated. The last major waterfront settlement was even more discouraging. In November 1971, a fifty-eight-day strike, during which numerous ships were diverted to Canadian ports, was ended by a court order. Its most important accomplishments were to raise wages to $5.50 an hour and make it evident that an optimum solution to Boston's labor-management problems was yet to be found.

The Port's labor future rests upon meeting two requirements: the employment of the labor force at a level of efficiency that will ensure economic use of valuable port equipment and the satisfaction of the needs of the Boston longshoremen so that the labor unions will accept such a policy.[10] The unions must exercise wise leadership and impress upon their members the self-defeating consequences of a vicious cycle in which inefficiency leads to greater costs and hence reduced traffic. The rank and file must abide more discipline in port operations. Boston labor should follow the example of the West Coast, where, as early as 1960, a Mechanization and Modernization Agreement was reached due to the progressive union leadership of Harry Bridges of the Pacific Maritime Association, who recognized that port efficiency can benefit the unions as well as management. As for Boston management, in order to make port modernization viable, management must recognize the right of labor to jobs or monetary compensation, although this approach may be repugnant to traditional business disciples.

Opportunities for specific reforms abound in Boston's labor picture. Some recommendations that have been put forward include genuine changes in work rules and practices to permit decasualization, labor flexibility, and better use of manpower. An open union and an intensive training program would stabilize employment, improve wage practices and working conditions, and increase productivity. Labor morale could be advanced by steady work conditions, appropriate pier equipment, and productivity bonuses. Finally, a mandatory retirement age and generous pension benefits for longshoremen and clerks would enhance the character of Boston's labor force. Though inumerable suggestions could be offered within this general outline of the Port's labor predicament, a few more precise issues will be discussed in a later section on containerization.

## Competition with New York

The port of New York has played as important a role in Boston's maritime history as any of the Port's various indigenous components. It has competed with and dominated Boston for well over a century. It has been an acknowledged prototype and an accused manipulator. Its influence, both visible and invisible, proper and improper, has been recently on the rise. Though of late losing ground for the first time relative to other U.S. ports, New York may be as decisive a determinant of the future of the Port of Boston as any other single factor.

The futility of Boston's competition with New York was already apparent in the 1830s as the coveted business of the western hinterland concentrated in New York. This role as a centralized distribution point has been strengthened over time since few individual trades are sufficiently large to support scheduled and frequent sailings, and service must increasingly be on a regional basis. The spread of containerization, with increased investment and operating costs, has only exacerbated this situation. Along the U.S. North Atlantic coast, Boston, along with Philadelphia, Baltimore, and Hampton Roads, is an outport or fringe-port, overshadowed by New York, the premier regional and national port. Enjoying the luxuries of a great international commercial center, New York attracts huge volumes of diversified cargo and a multitude of vessels from every corner of the globe. Meanwhile, Boston struggles to remain a viable regional port and must constantly and anxiously compete with its voracious neighbor that threatens to deprive it of even its local New England customers.

New York has always been more advanced and aggressive than Boston and, hence, better prepared to adapt to innovations, both technological and institutional. In contrast to Boston's belated and faltering exertions, it had the capacity to promptly and vigorously exploit the railroad, the steamship, containerization, and a new concept of port administration. The Port of New York Authority, a joint venture of the states of New York and New Jersey, was established in 1921 and has successfully operated the port without interruption since then. It has had a half century to acquire expertise and experience, develop organization and policy, and learn to effectively exercise increased responsibility and power. During the same period, the Port of Boston has been administered by five different agencies; the present one, Massport, the only truly autonomous, corporate authority, was modeled after the Port of New York Authority and is still a relative adolescent. The Port of New York Authority, blessed with great internal revenues, has been able to maintain, with no external funding, a general Reserve Fund equal to at least 10 percent of its total debt for continuous capital investment. Massport, on the other hand, has had to rely on revenue bonds for investment capital and, only recently, has undertaken a major port improvement program. Even with this, the scales of respective projects are almost embarrassing in comparison, as the Mystic Container Terminal pales before its counterpart, the immense Port Elizabeth, N.J., complex.

It is not difficult to understand why New York has been able to successfully capture and maintain 80 percent of New England's general cargo outbound traffic and 50 percent of its inbound traffic, the bulk of which should naturally flow through Boston. There are numerous and varied reasons that make New York a more attractive port than Boston. Boston has a reputation of labor difficulties, the highest loss and pilferage rates of any major U.S. port, and the highest cost structure and lowest labor productivity of any East Coast port. The Port consists of a proliferation of facilities, most outmoded and decrepit, scattered over miles of waterfront with congested and narrow access roads.

While New York's railroads, besides offering free and excellent lighterage service, absorb the costs of loading and unloading, the Boston carriers are the only lines in the North Atlantic that pass these costs on to shipper or consignee. Moreover, New York, as the hub of U.S. foreign and domestic waterborne commerce, is more able to sustain a higher level of charges without affecting its competitive position than is a secondary port like Boston. Port costs in Boston are only marginally lower than those in New York and, consequently, can't overcome other incentives for using the larger port.

Many feel that Boston can only compete if it can offer a more favorable cost structure and better waterfront services than New York; this is true to an extent. Recent Massport solicitation efforts centering around the lower tariffs offered by nonconference general cargo ships calling at the Port have met with moderate success in luring local firms from New York. Variations in cost, however, are rarely of decisive significance to most shippers and receivers in selecting a port. Steamship service is the single most important reason among New England manufacturers for choosing New York over Boston. Though able to realize considerable savings by using Boston, local businesses route their cargoes through New York because of the advantages of frequent and regular steamship schedules, an asset largely lacking in the home port. With the same price quoted Free Alongside Ship (F.A.S.), New York or Boston, a customer deciding a routing might also prefer expediting his business through New York despite higher inland freight rates. Another advantage in New York is traffic to and from infrequently served ports, such as several in South Africa with which New England firms are doing increasingly more business. Since Boston is customarily the first port of call and New York the last, Boston can compete for imports but not for those exports which it is always so sorely wanting. This is based largely upon the time elapsed between the date of readiness of cargo and the date of departure of that cargo on the overseas leg. Boston is in a relatively favorable position with respect to elapsed time on inbound services, but its outbound cargoes average a delay of 15.8 days before final departure compared to 2.0 days for New York.[11] Despite New York's truck congestion at piers and increased "lead" time for the movement of cargo, New England shippers will continue to use the port even if the extra land carrier charge is raised. It is possible that even more New England trade will pass through New York unless service into the Port of Boston is quickly and permanently improved.

In order to establish more frequently scheduled direct service, Boston will have to pursue a more aggressive program to attract new steamship lines to the Port. While it presently enjoys good service to Europe and the Mediterranean, Boston offers inadequate service to South America, with only one ship making the southbound run to Brazil. The current Sea Land service to the Caribbean is chronically prone to delays and rerouting and more reliable service is needed. Boston's service to the important Far East market is especially deficient, consisting, of consortium service once every seven weeks, a feeder line to Halifax, and only one line of combination vessels maintaining direct regular service. While the Far East run needs particular attention, liner service to most areas will have to be upgraded if Boston is not to lose even further ground to its arch rival, New York.

Feeding this not-so-friendly rivalry has been Boston's traditional xenophobia towards both Washington and especially New York. The local conviction that President Jefferson was out to destroy New England is paralleled today by Massport officials who have considered Boston's principal menace to be "a national maritime policy which dictated abandonment of the Boston Port in favor of concentrating shipping activities in other areas."[12] But the most intense suspicion is reserved for New York, whose supreme financial and social structure has always evoked a curiously defensive resentment on the part of proper Bostonians. Earlier, the Port had watched helplessly as its shipping lines and railroads gradually came under alien domination, if not control. This indignity was recently resurrected when New York flaunted the Shipping Act of 1916 and the Merchant Marine Act of 1920 which forbid the diversion of cargo from a natural tributary port to another. With dubious legality, several steamship companies and conferences began to absorb the additional overland freight charges for transporting cargo to and from New York, thus cutting even further into Boston's business. The strategy was ended only after a series of complaints by Massport to the Federal Maritime Commission in Washington and the U.S. Federal District Court in Boston.[13]

Many Bostonians feel that beneath such surface manifestations lies a conscious and covert intention to frustrate and even destroy the Boston seaport. There is a general conviction that the pressure and control of New York shipping interests has been one of the main contributions to the Port's decline:

The objective of the New York complex is to concentrate all major shipping activity in the New York area by forcing Boston out of the picture. New York shipping interests directly control most of the local factions which affect the maritime industry in Boston. They have total control over freight forwarders, agents, stevedores, ship scheduling and routing, labor policy or the lack of it, rail charges and other costs.[14]

Whenever Boston's maritime potential threatened to infringe on New York's convenient and profitable hegemony, the "big squeeze" was applied. This took the form of a program of diversions, delays, cancellations, and labor disputes that Boston's Port Director described as a "cycle of unfortunate conditions generated by New York maritime interests."[15] All Boston shipping companies are based in New York and many believe that the BSA is dominated by New York interests and that local labor is manipulated in accordance with New York's, rather than Boston's ambitions. Under these conditions, New York shipping companies are felt to have a powerful, if not controlling, voice in Boston's labor-management pacts. As objective an observer as the Federal Maritime Commission has noted that:

Many of the stevedores, steamship agents and freight forwarders in the Port of Boston are owned, operated or in some fashion controlled by firms in the Port of New York. New York control tends to affect managerial decisions in favor of the Port of New York, but the ultimate effects on the utilization of the Port of Boston has not been determined.[16]

Whether this general anxiety is based on exaggerated neurosis or experienced insight, its indirect influence on the Port of Boston cannot be denied. It will continue to have a strong and negative impact on Boston with or without the documentation of specific offenses. The conviction that the decision-making processes in the Port are not entirely independent would tend to dampen impulses toward imaginative and aggressive policies, and this state of affairs would only further demoralize the already insecure Boston maritime community.

**Constitution of the Port:
Containerization and Massport**

*This new development (automation) has unbounded
possibilities for good and for evil.*

Norbert Wiener

## Containerization

Containerization is one of the few relatively revolutionary concepts adopted by
the archly conservative shipping industry since the Phoenicians. It takes a simple
but novel approach to ocean conveyance as one integer in a rational and efficient system of transporting goods to and from inland sites, making optimal use
of the inherent advantages of several modes of transport. Marine transportation is now considered one phase of production and marketing with a premium
on an integrated scheme of production, overland transport, port terminal transfer, and seaborne carriage. This intermodal method was first looked to as the
miraculous, all-in-one solution to the stagnation of the Port of Boston. This
view may ultimately be justified; but as containerization takes root in Boston
it not only benefits from the Port's traditional assets and newly rediscovered
enthusiasm, but must also confront its notorious liabilities and entrenched dis-
position. As such, the introduction of intermodal transport in Boston approximates a fairly accurate microcosm of the Port's total character.

Containerization, like all industrial or institutional innovations, makes
demands that not all can meet and offers benefits that not all may enjoy. The
demoralized Boston shipping community of the 1960s was willing to grasp at
any straw and became convinced that the new technology would prove the
Port's panacea. While this attitude was somewhat Pollyannish, there are many
aspects of containerization that appeared attractively applicable to some of the
Port's dilemmas. With an emphasis on speed, Boston is favorably located 200
miles closer to Europe than any other U.S. North Atlantic port and can afford
shippers a 30¢ per ton differential on sea carriage. The local industrial high-
value–low-bulk products, especially small electrical and machinery components,
are easily and advantageously containerized. Containerization might permanently improve Boston's inadequate flow of exports by attracting both new shippers
and those New England firms that customarily use New York. Its minimization
of cargo loss, damage, and pilferage is ideal for Boston where such incidents were
rampant, and the subsequent lowering of insurance rates could ameliorate the
Port's high-cost reputation among shipping lines.

Most importantly, containerization can help revive the Port by attracting new steamship lines with frequent and regular schedules. It might even break tradition and make Boston a last port of call, thus offering exporters more direct outbound service. Furthermore, containerization will reduce the number of ships in port because of the more regular service, shorter port time, and larger cargo load per ship call. This would more quickly eliminate redundant and obsolete facilities that have yielded little utility while absorbing considerable funds for rehabilitation and maintenance. Intermodal transportation also promises to reduce freight rates by almost 50 percent, primarily by its own speed and efficiency and the minimal use of Boston's low-productivity labor force. The port director has estimated that the unloading of 2000 tons of break-bulk cargo would occupy five gangs for four days. With containers, the labor cost could be as low as one-sixth of that with conventional methods since the same unloading would require only two gangs and two cranes for eight hours.[1] Potential through billing and documentation could be expected to lower administrative costs. Finally, Boston's arrangement of inland transportation is generally well suited to the intermodal system. Boston has come to rely on the motor carrier as its primary means of overland transport because of its speed, dependability, flexibility, and reasonable freight charges. Though efficiency could be improved, there is sufficient truck service to satisfy any future demand, and superhighways connect the Port to virtually all points in the U.S. and Canada. Though underutilized, Boston's three railroads offer equally good service.

While all these obvious benefits from containerization were justifiably enticing to port management, there was little initial discussion of those facets of containerization that might be incompatible with Boston's defective maritime condition and even threatening to its development. These conspicuous disadvantages were as equally impressive and abundant as the presumed advantages of intermodal transportation. First of all, containerization accelerates the concentration of shipping in large regional ports, such as neighboring New York, as enlarged service areas are needed to generate sufficient cargoes and assure a more stable cargo flow. This process is inherent in the intermodal system: "The introduction of container ships, capable of carrying twice the cargo each sailing and of making two to three times as many sailings each year, will exacerbate the problem (insufficient freight) and emphasize the need in a very high proportion of the world's trades to approach scheduling regionally rather than on a bilateral basis."[2] Though many feel there is a need for several major container ports on the East Coast to account for labor closings, congestion, and alternate ports for military use, experience has shown that such ports often evolve into secondary, supporting facilities for a large primary port. So, Boston still finds itself in combat with Goliath New York, with even a possible increase in the vigor of the competition as an overcapacity in container port facilities seems certain. This competition is intensified by the magnified importance of exports, a rude fact Boston has hopelessly faced for years, since container ships are highly capital-intensive and demand full bottoms on both legs of a voyage. Since container cargoes are concentrated in larger lots, moreover, small shippers, who constitute the majority of local concerns using the Port of Boston, are placed at a disadvantage. Furthermore, consolidation and competition have resulted in a few very large container shipping lines with more power and control vested in fewer decision makers located in a handful of premier international ports.

A more internal disadvantage at the beginning was Massport's seemingly inflexible policy of immediate development of Logan Airport with minimal capital investment in the Port, and most of that appropriated for the rehabilitation of obsolete facilities. Large-scale containerization confronted this investment pattern with a demand for an extraordinary and direct application of funds, prodigious compared to prior port projects, in order to install the attendant sophisticated and specialized handling equipment. Equally important for the new intermodal scheme is that such specialization requires optimization of the total transport system. Though Boston had sufficient truck and rail services at hand and occupied a central location as to major highways, its important feeder lines were inefficient due to narrow and confined access roads, many remote from major arteries and consolidation areas. Furthermore, Boston did not have the advanced control mechanism that is an absolute prerequisite for a profitable container operation. Port activities were accustomed to lumbering along with no coordination of facilities and an inadequate organization and separation of cargo and vehicular flow.

The most obvious incompatibility, however, was between Boston's waterfront labor with its notoriety for rock-bottom productivity, delaying tactics, and time consumption and container ships that demand an ultrarapid turnaround time in order to justify their large capital investment and operating costs. An efficient, productive, reliant, semi-skilled labor force is mandatory for successful intermodal operation, and Boston could not even assume pretenses on any of these counts.

Despite these obstacles, containerization encountered an uncritically receptive atmosphere in Boston where Massport and most shipping interests were convinced that it presented a unique opportunity for the long stagnant port. A comprehensive study of the Port's market potential and development requirements was completed for Massport in 1964 by the New York firm of Rowland and MacNeal; its findings supported the intuitive optimism of the local shipping community, and it strongly recommended the complete modernization of the Port. The results of this study prompted Massport to firmly commit itself to containerization; soon afterwards, the Authority hired a new port director, Thomas Soules, to specifically implement the report's recommendations.

Although containerization was now definitely in Boston's future, its introduction was predictably prolonged and troublesome, keeping in character with the Port's traditional mode of adopting technological developments. At the time, Massport was spending heavily on Logan Airport and lacked the investment capital necessary for any elaborate, initial effort at containerization. Instead, it embarked on a small-scale venture that proved ill-advised and counterproductive. In June 1966, it completed construction of a $1.25 million, 27.5 ton gantry crane at Castle Island and, as prearranged, leased the crane, one berth, and ten acres of land to Sea Land Inc. for twenty-five years for over $2.4 million. This move was expected to begin the revitalization of the Port of Boston. At first, this seemed to be the case, as Sea Land's activities spurred other companies to improve their service to Boston and plan for their own container operations in the Port. U.S. Lines quickly leased space from the New York Central Railroad in front of Pier 1 in East Boston for container handling and storage.

The promise, however, turned into a fiasco, with inevitable labor difficulties as the catalyst. The scheduled inauguration of container services at Boston was postponed because of differences between the ILA and the BSA. The union demanded seven clerks as at Port Elizabeth and the shippers would concede only three. Finally, the issue, along with several others, was resolved in the 1966 agreement described earlier.

No sooner had the dust settled, however, than the local teamsters entered on the scene and demanded the right to move trailers between the marshalling area and shipside and insisted that two additional teamsters be employed as mechanics inside the terminal, both functions normally performed by the ILA in New York. This jurisdictional dispute proved impossible to resolve at the local level, and the controversy was sent to higher headquarters in New York in the fall of 1967.

Not long after ILA President Thomas W. Gleason and Teamster President James Hoffa reached an accord over these differences, Boston was plunged into a nationwide strike. On April 2, 1969, the 104 day strike, the longest and costliest ever, was settled. It had cost the Port of Boston about $15 million in diverted shipping and lost labor time. Behind the subsequent 1969 labor-management pact, the only modernized agreement in the Port for years, was ILA President John Moran's ultimate conviction that labor, for its own long-term sake, must cooperate with technological advances in port operations. It was an expensive lesson for all sides, but seemed auspicious for further containerization.

Boston lost more than port revenues because of these labor tribulations. They prompted many important European lines that had initially been attracted by the prospect of containerization, such as Isbrandsten, to turn to New York where extensive container development was proceeding quickly and with minimal labor problems. A further blow to the Port in its competition with New York was the consolidation of four major European lines — Holland-American, Swedish-American, Cunard, and Wallenius — into the giant Atlantic Container Line headquartered at Port Elizabeth. The Port's labor difficulties along with a general retrenchment among American container companies led U.S. Lines to close its Boston office and, after unsuccessfully attempting to get out of the container business altogether, concentrate on operations focusing around New York and Norfolk.

Throughout this burlesque of progress, Sea Land insistently professed that the two principal reasons for its postponing operations at Castle Island were labor problems and its shortage of available ships due to the logistics of the Vietnam conflict. Sea Land did not mention that its Vietnam business was more lucrative than any Boston could offer. The veracity of both rationalizations was impaired, however, after the labor situation was stablized and U.S. Far Eastern activities began to wind down. Sea Land still, inexplicably, gave no indication of initiating operations. Finally, in July 1970, the Castle Island terminal began service, four long years after its completion. Soon, one ship arrived weekly to unload and load 200 to 250 containers for the North Atlantic, Puerto Rican, and intercoastal trades. Not long thereafter, however, Sea Land announced the closing of its Castle Island terminal. The company claimed the $1 per container surcharge it was required to contribute to the longshoreman's pension fund made Boston more expensive to operate in than other North Atlantic ports. It took three weeks of negotiation among Sea Land, the ILA, and the BSA before an agreement was reached whereby Sea Land could assess a usage fee to offset the surcharge.

These shipping antics, while amusing to a detached observer, had serious consequences as container traffic was increasingly diverted from Boston to New York and the process of concentration, which although possibly unavoidable, was accelerated. Many in Boston's shipping community saw these developments less as a confluence of natural forces and more as the habitual machinations of its gluttonous rival to the south. They felt that the Port could have established itself as a leading container center if not for "foreign" instigation of delays, labor troubles, and frustrations. Some felt containers were induced to move through New York by the "questionably legal means" of absorbing the higher overland freight charges to New York for New England cargoes.[3] Others hinted that the President of the BSA, a branch manager of the New York based U.S. Lines, was "somehow responsible" for the Port's labor disputes and delayed settlement. Finally, even Sea Land was cast as a villain. One explanation that gained local favor as to why the Castle Island terminal was not used was that Sea Land was protecting its real interests in its major container facilities in New York. By retaining exclusive rights to Boston's only container terminal with no commitment to use it, the company could in effect control, at least temporarily, competition to its New York operations from the Port of Boston. This design was enhanced by the fact that the Boston facility was built to a size module that would not fit containers of other shipping companies.[4] Unfortunately, Boston relied too heavily on the good intentions of Sea Land, and Castle Island will remain contractually committed to the company until 1991.

Despite these frustrations, Massport was convinced more than ever that the Port's future lay in increased containerization and proceeded with plans for an extensive new facility in Charlestown. Encouraged by the 1969 labor contract on port modernization, which seemed to assure a dependable labor force, and the prospect of expanded containerization of the Port, many of the shipping lines that had earlier abandoned Boston were attracted back. Four container lines began regular service from Europe, the Mediterranean, and the Far East and a fifth planned service from Australia and New Zealand as soon as expanded facilities were offered. In contrast to these optimistic signs on the horizon, Massport ran into unforeseen trouble at home. The Port Authority, as is its custom, had failed to consult with other local government agencies about its container program, and the construction of the Charlestown terminal soon erupted in a public row with the Boston Redevelopment Authority (BRA). At the same time Massport was pursuing containers, public support was mounting for alternative utilization of harbor resources for urban renewal and recreation. As champion of this cause, the BRA claimed Massport was operating in an urban renewal area and was endangering a larger development plan without coordinating or clearing its plans with the BRA.[5] Although the BRA's indignation and opposition were predestined to futility given Massport's autonomy and indifference, the incident nevertheless tarnished Massport's already mottled public relations image.

Anticipation of the new project continued unabated, however, and hopes for port rejuvenation abounded. In the early summer of 1971, Massport could confidently state: "Although general cargo has been declining, it got worse more slowly in 1970. This year will be the turning point. The opening of the world's largest container crane in early July will produce a dramatic increase in tonnage."[6] Soon thereafter, Massport's first major capital investment in the Port came to fruition. In July 1971, the Boston-Mystic Public Container Terminal (later renamed the John F. Moran Terminal in honor of the deceased ILA President) began operations under Massport. The $25 million, 45-acre terminal has 1100 feet of berth space. The 70-ton Hitachi crane is the world's largest capacity dockside general purpose and container crane and is supplemented by a 45-ton capacity Paceco container crane. Together, the cranes can move up to sixty containers an hour from one or two vessels. The exultant greeting for this new port addition can only be compared with the premature rhetoric that followed the lifting of the railroad rate differential in 1963. John Larkin Thompson, former Port Authority chairman saw Boston facing "probably the single greatest maritime opportunity in 50 years."[7] Edward Dalton, New England Vice President of the ILA, more prosaically stated, "We're back in the ball game."[8]

So far, these claims do not appear to have been overly exaggerated, as the dramatic increase in container traffic in Table 6-1 indicates. The trend in fact seems to be accelerating; the Moran Terminal handled 271,412 tons through August 1974, for a 62 percent increase over the tonnage for the same period in 1973. More promising, containerization has succeeded in attracting increased exports to Boston and is the prime reason overall general cargo exports leaped

**Table 6–1**
**Container Traffic Through the Port of Boston**

| Year | Container tonnage (Expressed in short tons) | | | Containers handled (Expressed in twenty-foot equivalent units) | | |
|------|----------|----------|---------|----------|----------|--------|
| | Imported | Exported | Total | Imported | Exported | Total |
| 1971 | 211,519 | 144,799 | 356,318 | 22,704 | 19,768 | 42,472 |
| 1972 | 298,139 | 159,664 | 457,803 | 35,170 | 24,424 | 59,594 |
| 1973* | 394,692 | 218,561 | 613,253 | 43,470 | 30,513 | 79,983 |

*Figures supplied by Massachusetts Port Authority.
Source: Massachusetts Port Authority 1973 Annual Report.

from 89,000 tons in 1972 to 153,000 tons in 1973.[9] For 1974, all indications were that Boston would have the best shipping year yet and that container imports and exports would be nearly balanced, an auspicious milestone in the Port's short history of containerization. All North Atlantic ports have shared this rise in exports due to a marked increase in the demand for American products overseas which stems from the devaluation of the dollar in mid-1973. This shift in trade patterns is reflected in the 1973 U.S. $1.7 billion surplus in its import-export balance, thereby reversing a trend of several years.[10] This abundance of exports also resulted from a period of domestic price controls that made exports more attractive and induced many American firms to open overseas offices to escape these restraints. In Boston, these factors have produced the unique situation of export cargo growing at a pace faster than the shipping lines can cope with. The president of a leading Boston shipping agency has said, "We are at the point now where you cannot get space on some runs for six weeks. There just are not enough ships to handle the growth of cargo."[11]

This abundance of freight must also be credited to the success of Massport's vigorous and extensive solicitation efforts. While it has made some inroads in upper-state New York, Massport currently feels the Midwest is too uncertain an area for serious solicitation, primarily because of unfavorable inland rates, and Boston consequently receives only a trickle of containers from the far hinterland. Massport has been very effective, however, in enticing New England shippers back from the port of New York. It has concentrated its solicitation efforts in New England, where Boston enjoys a truck rate advantage, and feels very confident about future business from Massachusetts, Rhode Island, and Maine. Connecticut still remains tentative and Massport, while conceding the southern section to New York, feels that northern Connecticut should avail itself of Boston's lower truck rates and has made this area its main solicitation target. Massport has also assisted in establishing a promising consolidation system at Moran for Less than Container Loads (LCLs) to offer the maximum benefits of containerization to the many small local shippers who otherwise would use New York. It is even proffering to local liquor and bottling concerns an imaginative method of containerizing scotch whiskey and European wines to the disgruntlement of thirsty dockworkers. Massport has been rewarded for its efforts by a marked improvement in both cargo volume and steamship service to the Port. A total of twenty-four regularly scheduled lines call on Boston, five carriers of which are on a weekly basis. Other ships are attracted to the Port on an "inducement basis" dependent on the needs of local shippers.

Less encouraging has been the local labor reaction which has not been as stable as was hoped. There has been one major strike and productivity is not yet optimum as the longshoremen have not completely abandoned their old work habits. Boston is developing a more reliable, semi-skilled labor force, however, which has even been willing to work nights for the first time in the Port's history when cargo volume demanded it.

The terminal itself has already been operationally improved. A control tower similar to those at airports has been erected to coordinate activities through a communications system linked to the ships, the cranes, and the marshalling carriers. A fully computerized inventory control system was inaugurated, in June 1974, to maximize efficiency, speed of handling, and security.

Despite this encouraging start, the Moran Terminal has experienced its share of difficulties. Trucking problems have become apparent with a great need for more chassis and premounted containers and improved coordination of truckers' hours and terminal operating hours. The terminal has also suffered equipment failure stemming from overuse, and there is general agreement that it lacks sufficient management personnel. Furthermore, an excess of paperwork has resulted in inefficiency and costly delays. Hopefully, eventual passage of intermodal legislation by Congress will alleviate this last problem through the licensing of intermodal carriers by the Federal Maritime Commission and the establishment of single-factor rates under a through bill of lading.

The major defect of the Moran Terminal, however, is that short-sighted planning located it on a site that presents inherent and irresoluble limitations. Situated on Massport's Mystic Wharf, it is about four miles from the mouth of the inner harbor; passage to the terminal requires several sharp turns; and the Mystic River channel is too narrow to provide a good turning basin. These factors make for difficult navigation and have already resulted in higher rates for tug service; combined with depth limitations, they may in the future prevent access to the terminal by the new generation of larger container vessels.

The greatest problem at Moran, however, is that it reached its capacity three years earlier than expected and is now experiencing serious congestion due to a lack of adequate truck marshalling and storage areas. There has been criticism that the facility is actually operating at only about one-half of its equipment handling capacity and that the really pressing need is for expanded land space, a problem that could have been avoided with more provident planning. When Massport completes construction for the second berth at Moran, the facility will require forty-five-acres of backup space to efficiently handle its projected capacity of 50,000 tons a year, a capacity that many feel is unrealistic given practical operating restraints. Currently, the terminal occupies only about twenty-two acres and Massport is attempting to ameliorate the glaring deficiency. It has contracted with Schiavone and Sons., Inc., a scrap metal exporter abutting the terminal, for the future reacquisition of eight acres of land and is negotiating with the Boston & Maine Railroad for an additional eleven acres of their property on Mystic Wharf. The completion of the second berth and the eventual expansion of Moran's storage and operating space, however, entails at best an unsatisfactory delay and, in any case, will not ultimately meet the projected demand for container handling beyond the immediate future.

As it became increasingly apparent that the Moran terminal would not be able to accommodate the expanded flow of container business that was hoped for and expected, Massport began to plan for an additional facility. It contracted C. E. Maguire Inc. to prepare an economic and engineering evaluation of the need and feasibility of another container terminal for Boston. The study was completed in late 1973 and confirmed that the projected demand for containerization would be beyond the Port's current handling capacity. The Maguire report also confirmed the poor planning that went into the Moran Terminal. It found that further expansion of the facility beyond what was presently underway was impractical. It indicated that an enlarged, four berth facility would require an additional eighty-five-acres of backup area, practically the entire Mystic Wharf land space. Total development of Moran would entail displacing the private operations of the U.S. Gypsum Co., the Boston & Maine Railroad, and the Wiggins Terminal, consolidating the Schiavone scrap operations, and filling in three general cargo piers. The study could not recommend such a massive impact on other users of the wharf. The Maguire report concluded that an additional container facility would be required after 1976 and that Massport's existing thirty-five-acre East Boston terminal would be the most suitable site. The new facility was estimated to cost approximately $39 million and require at least four years to design and construct. Once announced, Massport's plan was hailed by labor as "the salvation of the Port" and considered by all interested parties to be "almost a certainty."[12]

Though Massport's plan demonstrated commendable initiative and was supported by all port interests, it soon stirred up a quite predictable controversy. To implement its program in East Boston, a community already suffering the presence of Logan Airport, Massport had to turn reluctantly to its old sparring partners at the BRA and request a delay in their plans for a $3.1 million housing project for the elderly and a new zoo. This apparent callousness sparked local outrage; and, before long, there was vociferous protest from the residents of

East Boston who feared, among other things, that the proposed terminal would dangerously increase truck traffic, disrupt the community, and pave the way for further encroachment by Massport. Opponents of the plan gained powerful editorial support from the sympathetic Boston press: "East Boston has been battered enough already by its huge neighbor. To impose a container terminal, for whatever practical reasons, on this piece of waterfront would be humanly shameful and aesthetically destructive."[13]

Massport strategically retreated and soon produced a controversial supplemental study that reassessed the situation and now indicated the South Boston Naval Annex as a better site than the East Boston location originally suggested by the primary study. Massport had hoped to avoid having to seek the South Boston site since it would involve considerable capital expenditure for land acquisition and public competition with other potential users of the facility. Negotiations with city, state, and federal officials are necessary since the Annex is soon to be disposed of as military surplus. Nevertheless, by an overwhelming vote, Massport's Board authorized the executive director to seek the 220-acre South Boston site for a container facility. Although Massport has become more than willing to trade the city its East Boston property for the South Boston location, a proposed shipyard for the Annex offers the greater inducement of increased employment and property taxes. Furthermore, a Special Legislative Commission on Boston Harbor, headed by the same state senator who instinctively opposes Massport at every turn, may soon be moving into the area of development control modeled after the San Francisco Bay Commission.

Despite these current frustrations, the Boston shipping community remains very optimistic about the Port's containerized future and supports Massport's efforts of expansion. It foresees a growth in the North Atlantic trade and, with Yankee pragmatism, views the eventual saturation of these routes after 1975 as a good opportunity to establish new container routes to Brazil and South Africa, areas with which Boston is cultivating increased business. Meanwhile, Massport has made its decision and publicly committed itself to further containerization of the Port. Given Massport's past history and independent character, it will probably pursue this policy regardless of local friction, increasingly concentrated competition in New York, and the problematic future of the possibly overcapitalized and overcapacitized container trade.

## Massport

Boston is one of the most fragmented ports in the United States, with a proliferation of associations, agencies, and trade organizations. Amid this crowded community, however, the Massachusetts Port Authority has maintained the highest profile and been the center of port activity since beginning operations in 1959. It has been and will continue to be embroiled in controversies, both petty and significant. Moreoever, Massport, in and of itself, has become a controversy, periodically evoking proposals for its replacement by a Waterfront Commission, a Metropolitan Port Commission, a New England Port Authority, or some such renovated body. This section shall briefly review some of the Port Authority's more consequential actions or inactions and suggest appropriate frames of reference for assessing the Authority's performance. It will be assumed that Massport will weather most storms of criticism fairly intact though probably modified in response to external pressure and will continue to guide the Port of Boston into the foreseeable future.

For a proper perspective, one must recognize the veritable credibility chasm between Massport's self-image and its public image among its steadfast opponents, as well as the general indifference shared by the greater part of the populace. Massport's staff sees itself as a small, dedicated group of honest, hardworking professionals expertly carrying out their delegated responsibilities. In contrast, the impression of the Port Authority among many local citizens is that it is powerful, arrogant, and self-serving; does not care about people or communities; cannot be trusted; and seldom, if ever, acts in the real public interest. Most Massachusetts residents are little affected by Massport and, consequently, little concerned about its activities.

To properly assess the first contradiction, it will be useful to approach it within the framework of a rough categorization of the three major channels of criticism. These are really only the more obvious facets of a complex web and are almost always interrelated, but they do offer a semblance of delineation. The three channels are:

1. Massport's administration of the Port
2. Its structural character
3. The concepts underlying its establishment and operations

*Administration*

Massport's administrative record elicits two general opinions prevalent among Boston's shipping community. One view is that Massport's administrative excellence has generated substantial economic growth and made it the most efficient and profitable public agency in the state. A contrasting estimation is that Massport's neglectful management has been inefficient and ineffective and has endangered the Port's very existence. Behind this criticism is the valid accusation that Massport has never attempted to design and implement a comprehensive long-range plan for the Port's revival and development: "The port management's piecemeal, haphazard approach to operations has encouraged inefficient work practices by the longshoremen, induced pessimism in the shippers and operators, and endangered long term profits."[14] Massport has certainly been deficient in this respect, not just with the seaport, but with Logan Airport as well. It may be that the Port Authority is more comfortable with this approach so it can keep its opponents off balance not knowing what, when, or where the next contentious project will be. Unfortunately, for whatever reasons, there are no assurances that Massport, on its own initiative, will significantly modify its characteristic approach and devise and publicize a concrete, coherent plan for the Port's future.

Containerization, which has recently been so vigorously introduced in the Port, does not necessarily denote a meaningful implementation of a viable, long-term development scheme, as evidenced by the miscalculated Moran Terminal and the awkward efforts to locate a new terminal. While containers may not indicate a master plan for the Port, they do, however, represent a constructive and consistent direction in which Massport has committed the Port and may bode well for the future. Meanwhile, barring any unforeseen political, financial, or legal rearrangements, Massport will continue in its more or less piecemeal fashion to the detriment of the Port of Boston and its factions, the local communities and their residents, and the state and its transportation system.

Another administrative target of criticism has been the persistent conviction that Massport has neglected the seaport in favor of concentrating almost exclusively on the development of Logan Airport. This early neglect cannot be denied, but, in retrospect, it was predictable and probably inevitable given Massport's fiscal structure and objectives. As explained in Chapter 2, the absence of supplementary funding, the requirements in Massport's enabling legislation for the diversion of port profits, and the nature of revenue bond financing made capital investments for port development difficult and unattractive. Massport's interim program of rehabilitating obsolete, decrepit, redundant facilities, however, was an inexcusable waste of money and an obviously ill-conceived makeshift exercise.

In recent years, however, investments for port projects have been increasing, culminating with the $25 million Moran Terminal; this trend will probably continue and even accelerate if Massport pursues its plans for a second, larger public container facility and an offshore oil terminal. This constructive shift in emphasis may indicate a new attitude on the part of Massport towards its revenue bond system. The general premise has been that Massport felt its primary responsibility to be towards its bondholders and, consequently, sought those available investments that assured an optimum return and avoided those that entailed either a minimal return or a significant risk. This obviously translated into early development of the airport and relative neglect of the seaport. The substance of this policy may have been altered by the fact that investments in Logan are presently neither so urgently needed nor so profitable, while investments in containerization are not only needed but have proven to be sound. This new, more flexible approach to hitherto unacceptably insecure port investments may reflect a new realization by Massport: "Concern for bondholders in itself is not a bad thing; in fact, it is salutary insofar as it motivates careful planning and sober judgement. However, since bondholders receive fixed returns on their investment, it is improbable that they would strenuously oppose any coherent plan for development which assures sufficient revenue to meet interest and principal obligations. Satisfying bondholders or investors is an integral part of any development program and need not necessitate conservatism."[15]

General criticism has also been leveled at Massport's program of port modernization. Successful management in this and other areas is dependent upon making the correct decisions at appropriate times and following them with vigorous implementation. For years, Massport demonstrated consummate skill in always avoiding any major port decision that required serious implementation. More progress would certainly have been made with a more aggressive program for port development, and the long delay in adopting containerization was indicative of the Port Authority's damaging passivity. While it did make a small investment in the crane for Sea Land's Castle Island operation, this was not until 1966, by which time other North Atlantic ports were well along with dynamic and extensive containerization programs. It then sat back for three years while the Sea Land operation showed no signs of materializing, making no apparent effort to investigate the possibility of coercing Sea Land to make good its intentions or of installing an alternative user in the facility. The BSA and other port interests clamored for Massport to develop facilities as they saw rival ports consolidating most of the container trade. Even as late as 1967, Massport's executive director was voicing the necessity to get in on the container movement before the steamship companies established their routes but doing little about it. All the Port Authority was prepared to do at that late date was to "stand ready to supply operational talents if needed or financial means where circumstances and a responsible leasee so warrant."[16] It was not until 1969 that Massport was convinced to take action. The "resolution" of two longstanding problems prompted the Authority to praise the year as "one of the most significant in the long history of the Port of Boston and certainly the most important year in the last two decades."[17] Not only was a new labor contract signed, but "the decision was made to proceed with the planning and development of a major public container and general cargo complex to be located on the Mystic River."[18]

It is still too early to say whether Boston jumped on the container bandwagon in time to realize the full complement of potential benefits that the intermodal revolution could provide. If nothing else, however, the first admittedly belated container terminal may, in retrospect, mark a watershed. Massport seems to have taken on a more aggressive stance since then, and plans for a larger public terminal and an offshore oil complex, while not tactfully initiated, may hopefully signify a more consistent and enterprising port development program.

The final two points of management criticism involve the critical areas of labor and solicitation. One of the most glaring weaknesses in the Port's structure is the inability to genuinely resolve, for an extended period of time, the labor difficulties arising from the discomposure accompanying modernization. Though Massport has been scored for this condition, it in fact has no statutory authority under its enabling act to negotiate directly with labor. Though it is represented in BSA-ILA bargainings, many feel it would be the more appropriate primary negotiator because of the BSA's close ties with New York. Massport justifiably claims, however, that officially its hands are tied. The Port Authority itself finds this situation frustrating and would prefer to be either the primary negotiator or out of labor bargaining altogether.

Until the last few years, Massport's solicitation efforts have been validly assessed as insufficient and ineffective. Though this partly resulted from conditions over which Massport had no control, other incidents, such as the perfunctory solicitation of Midwest grain after the rate differential was lifted, illustrated the Authority's lack of enthusiasm. Efforts were inadequate, fragmented, uncoordinated, and did little to present a consistent, positive image. This too, however, has greatly improved since Massport has acquired a saleable product in containerization. It has launched a full-scale, integrated, and sustained port promotion program and hired effective individuals to implement it. Branch offices have been improved or newly opened in Washington, D.C., New York, Chicago, Brussels, and Tokyo, and solicitation for cargo has been especially productive in New England and even New York state. Again, containerization may be ushering in a new era for Massport.

*Structure*

The administrative, financial, and political structure of Massport has probably been more controversial than its port operations and has certainly been more imposing and, in some cases, even threatening. More often than not it elicits a strong reaction, whether intimidation, admiration, or acrimony, from those that confront it. It has been appropriately likened to a fiefdom with a "closed system" of internal operation with little or no external interference or direction. The Board of Directors of Massport are part-time and unpaid, and none are professional port administrators. This arrangement has allowed effective power to devolve to the staff, with most of that power concentrated around the executive director. The present executive director, appointed in 1963, is the highest paid public official in the Commonwealth at $54,500 per year, beating even the governor and the U.S. senators. He is revered by the business community, depicted as "power-hungry" by his critics, and does indeed rule a self-contained entity often justly accused of a narrow, self-serving perspective.

Massport's broad power base is firmly rooted in Boston's commercial establishment. Financial and business leaders played a key role in Massport's creation, at a time when a crumbling transportation system endangered their profits.

They have shared in the benefits of the Port Authority's success and continue to have a vested interest in its operational and fiscal activities. Massport's revenue structure and its accountability to bondholders give it much in common with private enterprise, and the composition of its seven-man board, always consisting primarily of leading businessmen, serves to further strengthen this affinity.

Along with striving for business-like efficiency, Massport also respects the motivation for political reform that was crucial to its establishment. It was hoped that such a quasi-independent body, devoted to the public interest, would be removed from the possibility of political corruption and petty local interests. Massport has taken this responsibility seriously and values its untainted reputation in this respect. In context, this characteristic is all the more admirable: "The Authority has developed and maintained this 'good government' image in a state alleged to have widespread municipal corruption, where scandals are almost a way of life. Nothing in our research has led us to dispute the prevailing belief that the MPA is remarkably free from the crasser forms of venality that seem to plague so many other public bodies."[19] There has been anxious speculation, on the other hand, about the potential power and influence Massport could wield for unethical purposes if it were so inclined. The Port Authority could certainly draw on impressive and corruptive resources, such as its multi-million dollar finance system, its official and unofficial ties with commercial potentates, and the control it exercises over numerous employment opportunities and lucrative construction contracts. This potential danger, however, seems unavoidable in any large public authority that is fiscally autonomous and functions much like a private enterprise. Massachusetts, as with any other state, cannot have the best of both worlds. It has gotten, to a fair extent, the improved transportation facilities it had originally wanted but now finds a behemoth in its backyard that makes some people very uncomfortable. Massport has not yet abused its status but rather has policed itself much more effectively than most public agencies. While this is a situation the public should expect rather than applaud, realistically the Commonwealth has little complaint with Massport's self-conscious incorruptibility.

While Massport has chosen not unethically to flex its muscles, it has had no reservations, despite the naive hopes of many of its initial advocates, about amassing socially acceptable, legitimate political power. It is considered by many as the most powerful public organization and most effective political force in the Commonwealth. Massport has learned to play politics like a pro with three paid lobbyists; an extensive patronage list; and the judicial dispensation of jobs, Christmas gifts, harbor cruises, and airplane accommodations. There is often political motivation behind its board appointments and it has been often noted that "a combination of business savvy and politics has never proved to be an obstacle to appointment."[20] Massport has more than enough political clout to take the offensive for what it considers a good cause.

The Port Authority's defensive ability has proven equally potent and has earned it the reputation of being politically untouchable. Several hundred bills to change Massport or make it more responsive to local communities have been introduced in the state legislature only to die from lack of support. Most of these measures originate in the immediate Boston area, provoked by airport expansion; noise, air, and water pollution; waterfront decay; and traffic congestion. Massport dismisses these as "special interest" bills that don't merit general support, as it also dismisses a legislator's intemperate remarks as a political gesture necessitated by an election campaign in an embittered neighborhood. Massport feels no great threat from these sources; it sagaciously realizes that the vast majority of the populace is perfectly content with or indifferent to its operations as long as taxes are not affected. Consequently, it is fairly well immune from outside interference: "In sum, the main channel that the MPA's enabling legislation leaves open for reforming the Authority is blocked by the majority of the General Court that is not concerned with the MPA unless it affects their constituency directly."[21]

Many people, having little confidence in the legislature, feel that Massport should be more responsive to the governor. Governor Sargent himself stated that "when the actions of the Port (Authority) have major impact beyond the boundaries of the airport and affect many other interests of our people, then the public must be involved in those decisions, and I as governor will insist that the people have a say in those decisions."[22] The governor, however, failed to acquire a significant voice in shaping the policies and direction of Massport. Several attempts to give his office veto power over major Massport projects suffered defeat in the legislature. After the latest defeat, the bill's sponsor, a senator from East Boston, conceded that "The only explanation is that the bondholders (banks) just had too much clout with the Republicans and Ed King (of the P.A.) and the lobbyists with many of the Democrats."[23] Governor Sargent also looked to board appointments as a means of controlling Massport and integrating it into a statewide, balanced transportation program. Despite the fact that five members of the seven-man board were his appointees, the governor did not gain a handle on Massport. He could only muse: "It seems that any person appointed to that board is mesmerized by its power and strength. . . once they get into the clutches of the power, they forget about this office."[24]

The governor has not been alone in feeling isolated from the Port Authority, which has appeared to deliberately minimize its contacts with all other state agencies. Massport's structural independence has also meant an inconsistent relationship with the city of Boston, the level and sincerity of communications frequently dependent on the attitudes and policies of whoever is mayor at a given time. Massport has also neglected to coordinate its land development plans and activities with those of other agencies, in particular the Boston Redevelopment Authority whose relations with the Port Authority have been consistently strained.

If Massport's studied and cherished autonomy resulted only in bureaucratic frustrations, it could be dismissed as simply another provocation for typical political infighting. Regrettably, it has much more serious consequences. Massport's abstention from efforts to develop a comprehensive and coordinated transportation package for the entire state has had a damaging effect beyond the Authority's own dominion. Massport's indirect refusal to cooperate with other agencies severely hampers the planning and implementation of this much needed program. The intense passenger car and truck traffic generated by the airport and seaport would make attempts at even a revised metropolitan transportation system futile without the collaboration of the Port Authority. Massport claims it will study any "realistic plan" coming from the state Department of Transportation, but it is obvious that, for any plan to be realistic, Massport will have to participate more actively in its preparation and implementation. Massport's parochial reluctance to consider any framework other than its own sphere of influence was also demonstrated in its proposal for an offshore oil complex. The recent fuel shortage, if nothing else, has pointed out New England's common dilemma when it comes to energy production, distribution, and consumption. An offshore development program would entail a significant financial investment, affect the entire region's distribution pattern, and pose a considerable environmental hazard to the whole New England coast. In this perspective, anything but a regionally planned approach would be unwise and impractical; yet Massport persists with its characteristic individualism.

Unexpectedly, in the spring of 1973, Massport's obstinacy precipitated a confrontation that snowballed into the first real infringement on the Port Authority's autonomy. Massport's Board had held a midnight session to authorize a final bond issue to finance a $13.5 million, 2700-car parking garage at Logan Airport. In April 1973, Dr. William J. Bicknell, Commissioner of the Massachusetts Department of Public Health, advised Massport that its plans and specifications for the South Terminal project were required to be submitted to the Department's Bureau of Air Quality Control for review and approval under the state's Air Pollution Control Law. Massport held it was exempt from such regulations by the exclusionary provision in its enabling act. When asked his opinion, Attorney General Robert H. Quinn agreed with Massport's contention. The city of Boston ended up taking Massport to Superior Court, which decided that the legislative intent was that such bodies would not be subject to such regulations.

Soon thereafter, the Commonwealth was notified by the federal Environmental Protection Agency that "it appears that Massachusetts does not have the legal authority . . . to prevent the construction, modification or operation of State entities which will permit attainment or maintenance of a national standard" and that, if this "legal deficiency" was not corrected by September 1, 1973, over $1 million in federal grants would be cancelled.[25] The case was appealed to the Supreme Judicial Court, and, in March 1974, the Court rejected Massport's argument: "The consequence of the defendant's [Massport's] interpretation . . . of the [Port] Authority's enabling act would be that a small group of state authorities would have a unique exemption from the regulatory power of the state, an exemption available to no person or legal entity, public or private."[26]

This landmark decision not only makes Massport accountable to the Department of Public Health, but also, under the state's latest environmental protection law, it must now join the ranks of all other state agencies in assessing the environmental impact of any project it plans to undertake. Under this statute, adopted in 1972, Massport is required to submit an impact report to "all reviewing agencies, and any state agency, department, board, commission, division or authority which has jurisdiction by law or special expertise with respect to any environmental impact involved" for their written comments, including the secretary of environmental affairs, who will indicate if the report adequately and properly complies with the law.[27]

So Massport's first line of structural defense has been breached, and its privileged independence is no longer absolute. It will now be accountable to both its bondholders and the environment. It's far too early to tell what effect this will have on Massport's overall structure, policies, and operations. Hopefully, instead of begrudgingly cooperating with other state bodies, Massport will finally realize that it too has to be integrated into the broader governmental framework. The ruling will not so much affect Massport's efficiency and effectiveness as it will its self-image and philosophy as a body more corporate than public. Massport may even discover that there are valuable contributions to be made and received through interaction and collaboration with other public orginaizations.

*Concepts*

The final area of controversy revolves around the basic concepts underlying Massport's establishment and subsequent performance. The Port Authority was given a distinct and deliberate commercial orientation and has assiduously adhered to the business ethic in discharging its responsibilities. Though criticism of this approach has customarily focused on Logan Airport, it will probably be directed more towards the waterfront as Massport pursues a more active program of port development. This approach has been described as an "overriding emphasis on efficiency and profitmaking with respect to the facilities it was given to operate, which leads MPA management to function more like a private corporation than a public-regarding agency of government."[28] Despite its detractors, Massport has gratified its supporters and acquired a certain mystique because of its exemplary record of successful management and development.

One major reason for Massport's corporate success is that it finds itself in the enviable position of having the best of both worlds. As a quasi-public body, it enjoys many of the advantages of a public agency without the handicap of direct political accountability. It is not subject to periodic elections and, hence, is not directly accountable to the general citizenry. Moreover, its autonomous structure allows it to be equally exempt from responsibility to any other sector of the state government, legislative or executive, and this strengthens its immunity to most of the various internal restraints of democratic government.

This discretionary exercise of public prerogatives in corporate endeavors is a common problem inherent in most public authorities and is really at the heart of most conflicts over Massport's activities. The basic and often impassioned criticism is that Massport's evident interests do not conform with the broader public interest and that it is exclusively concerned with commercial prosperity and has little regard for other community values. It has been accused even by the BSA, its partner in maritime commerce, of having more allegiance to its bondholders than to the public.[29] A public relations study prepared for Massport itself cautioned that it "cannot be immune from a constructive response to growing public insistence that it be more concerned with the quality of life at its doorstep ... while continuing to improve the performance of its basic economic functions."[30] The same entrepreneurial success that instills admiration also aggravates criticism. Many believe that, while Massport exercises public power, it takes no account of the wider range of public needs and must be forced to adopt a more "holistic concept" of the public interest: "By the nature of its financial operations and political structure, the MPA is employing valuable public power — eminent domain (albeit restricted), the ability to sell tax-free bonds, exemption from local property taxes for most of its properties, appropriation of money collected from the public — in a way that might not be consistent with the public interest nor with a more rational and just ordering of social priorities."[31]

Massport is taken to account not only for pursuing ends not entirely compatible with the broader public interest, but also for the consequences of this pursuit. Massport's business orientation has in truth allowed and even encouraged it to ignore the social and environmental costs of its activities. There has been a persistent outcry against the direct effects of its operations on nearby users of land; these effects include air, noise, and water pollution; scenic degradation; the removal of recreational land; increased truck traffic; and impacts on local property taxes. Concern has also increased about the more general and obscure public consequences of the inequitable distribution of costs and benefits — financial and social — of Massport's operations and the disruptive role of these operations within the framework of an integrated metropolitan transportation strategy.

In fairness, however, the public must appreciate that Massport was established in effect as an advocate, and, despite the consequences of its narrow vision, it has devoted itself successfully to its cause, in particular the airport and, of late, the seaport. Its mandate was to take deteriorating transportation facilities and develop them into a system capable of meeting the demands of a dynamic commercial, industrial, and urban sector of the state. It was handed a mixed blessing in Logan Airport, the only major international airport located in such close proximity to a large metropolitan center, and this predicament has bred many controversies. All in all, Massport cannot be condemned for doing, to a good extent, what it was established to do, although the way it has gone about this is open to criticism.

Advocacy in public or quasi-public agencies is difficult at best but has become increasingly legitimate and necessary, as evidenced by government activities to protect the consumer, preserve the environment, and assist the elderly. These forms of advocacy are usually self-justified and readily accepted because they offer direct and visible benefits to the general public. As is often repeated, we are all consumers, we all share the same environment, and we all must eventually age. The advocacy assigned to Massport, however, is more contentious, for it requires a delicate technique to function effectively as this type of advocate without appearing a callous adversary. There are several reasons for this, not the least of which is the natural apprehension over endowing Massport with such imposing resources and discretionary power. A more subtle reason is that Massport's activities often appear unjustifiable because the general public only benefits indirectly, if at all. Although this is unavoidable with some of the Port Authority's undertakings, it does raise the larger question of development for development's sake. It seems, at times, that Massport has lost sight of its ultimate constituency, − i.e., the general public − and become too absorbed in its immediate constituents − i.e., the facilities themselves. This pitfall raises the further suspicion that Massport promotes development only to aggrandize more power for itself and that its facilities are only a means to this end. Massport has been accused of using Logan Airport in seeking power for the sake of power and may elicit similar reactions with offshore port development.

Whatever Massport's motivation, its development efforts for the Port must be viewed in a different light than those for Logan Airport. Since Logan is primarily used by a large segment of the general public, at least in the eastern part of the state, it constantly demonstrates its direct benefit to the public interest. The Port, meanwhile, is used by a small and exclusive group of shippers and consignees, and the general public is usually isolated from its functions. This naturally leads Massport to interpret the "public interest" solely in terms of the interests of its facility users. The benefits to the general public are, of course, much more indirect with this arrangement. Far fewer people, afterall, will ship a container than will board an airplane, even though containerization might improve the area's economic health and thus indirectly serve the public interest. These indirect, but often significant, benefits to the public interest do not justify Massport's frequent adversary posture or the regrettable consequences of some of its actions, but they must be appropriately considered in any assessment of the Port Authority's waterfront activities.

In this context, the public interest in the Port of Boston may actually have been better served by an earlier and more aggressive development program or, on the other hand, by a complete abandonment of the harbor to residential and recreational usage. Massport, as advocate for maritime interests, is committed to the indirect rather than the direct method of benefiting the general public. Although, at present, there is nothing really obnoxious about the Port's operations, it was to be expected that, as soon as Massport became more active on the waterfront, it would become a target of criticism from outside the shipping community. If Massport is required to recognize, assess, and justify the impact of its activities on both the communal and ecological environment, it may eventually incorporate these considerations in its overall orientation and begin to exhibit a new public consciousness and conscience. Port development can and should be more orderly and less contentious for Massachusetts than airport development has been. It may yet be that, in the end, as was planned in the beginning, all will benefit.

# 7

## Future of the Port

*Progress has not followed
a straight ascending line,
but a spiral with
rhythms of progress
and retrogression, of
evolutions and dissolution.*
                    Goethe

As a conclusion to this survey it would appear appropriate to conject upon the more conspicuous ingredients of Boston's maritime prosepcts, and to comment briefly on events too recent to have been incorporated into the main text. Boston's future horizons will be primarily determined by developments in the four areas that have recently been of most concern: modernization of the Port's petroleum reception facilities, further containerization of its general cargo-handling facilities, the uncertainty of the waterfront labor situation, and the role of the Massachusetts Port Authority within both the port structure and the state government. The components of these potential developments are numerous, varied, and often beyond local control — posing contingencies that preclude any confident predictions at this time. Nonetheless, since the interplay of these major factors will probably present more of the dilemmas with which the Port has customarily struggled, certain fundamental issues that will define the seaport's future are deserving of final note.

The development of an offshore oil terminal and refinery-industrial complex posed a serious quandry in a locale acutely sensitive to the preservation and protection of its natural environment. Despite a short burst of political support, Massport faced an uphill fight in suggesting replacement of a traditional supply system that was inconspicuously responsible for only a few oil spills beyond the inner harbor with one that would introduce carriers of such dimensions as to arouse anxieties about potential disasters of awesome magnitude and extent. In the end, the plan was dropped by the Port Authority Board. In the light of this eventual defeat, Massport's staff may have exhibited poor judgment in delaying for two years, while awaiting a more opportune moment, the presentation of its original offshore terminal study. If the staff was really convinced of the necessity for such a program, it should have assumed the responsibility of immediately publicizing the proposal as a high-priority issue for all of New England and undertaken an energetic campaign to recruit as much public, government, and industry support as possible. As it was, after a briefly receptive atmosphere, there proved to be too little visible need and sustained enthusiasm and too much publicized danger and entrenched opposition. A multitude of factors contributed to the plan's being dropped, not the least of which was a steadily growing insurgency by the Massport Board against Executive Director Edward King. Over the past several years, the board has been gradually acting with more independence after a long period of being generally dominated by its executive director. The board began asserting itself as the primary mechanism for policy and program decision making, and, although his customary autonomy was compromised, Executive Director King obediently abided by the board's decisions and carried out its directives. As a result of this, the board rejected a number of projects King had proposed and supported, including the deep-water port plan; many of these might otherwise have had a better chance of acceptance if the executive director's unilateral and vigorous advocacy had not been so effectively challenged.

There have been local and external developments, however, that were probably more decisive than Massport's internal politics in the failure of the offshore plan to gain adequate support. In contrast to earlier predictions of imminent and drastic problems, Boston's petroleum supply situation has actually improved somewhat. Oceangoing barges are not only efficiently maintaining the area's energy lifeline, but have also indefinitely extended the utility of the Port's inner-harbor oil terminals. There has also been an unanticipated decline in the growth rate for energy consumption in response to the repercussions from the price escalation of Middle East oil. Furthermore, as the prospects for Outer Continental Shelf oil extraction on Georges Banks are now more likely, New England may no longer be so entirely dependent for its energy needs on imported oil transported by tankers. Added to an improved supply prognosis is the encouraging fact that, with the implementation of the Federal Water Pollution Control Act Amendements, oil pollution along the eastern Massachusetts coastline has dropped dramatically. In 1974, there was a 75 percent decline in the amount of oil spilled by petroleum industry operations, including tankers, barges and terminals, and one freak truck accident which ruptured a north shore pipeline accounted for 71 percent of this total.[1]

There have also been many external developments to the Port which are affecting the nation's situation vis-à-vis supertankers and, in turn, have made offshore development appear a less urgent and necessary undertaking for Boston. Environmental concern over expanded use of supertankers has not abated, but rather has become, if anything, more entrenched as traumatic casualties continue and the increasing publicity attending them reduces earlier confidence that the VLCC–deep-water port system posed no unique ecological threat to the oceans. Complementing this spreading environmental intolerance has been a saturation of the supertanker market and an improvement in the prospects for smaller tankers. The supertanker trade has recently proven to be grossly overcapitalized with many vessels idled or laid up, construction contracts being cancelled, and owners accepting rockbottom charter rates just to keep vessels active and minimize their losses. On top of this, the opening of the Suez Canal means that "handy-sized" tankers of 30,000 to 100,000 tons will once again be economically feasible because of the reduced transit distance from the Middle East. The combination of these developments plus the presidential pocket veto of the Energy Transportation Security Act may blunt some of the impetus behind the proposed extensive construction of U.S. supertankers and shift the emphasis to smaller and more versatile vessels for the backbone of a modernized American tanker fleet.

Possibly the most consequential outside event for the Port of Boston was the passage of the Deepwater Port Act of 1974. Since the future use of supertankers may be reduced but will not be eliminated, this legislation was a necessary first step to expedite the development of modernized reception facilities to adequately and economically handle the anticipated increase in foreign petroleum imports. Plans have already been completed for deep-water ports off Louisiana and Texas, and it seems likely that a similar project will materialize soon for the Delaware Bay area. These facilities would make it possible to concentrate the flow of foreign imports in major regional centers and transship refined products to smaller ports in tankers or barges small enough to be accommodated. Hence it is feasible that New England could be indirectly guaranteed a supply of foreign petroleum without maintaining its own deep-water facility.

Offshore port development in some form is not an entirely dead issue for New England, however. Significantly more than one-half of the area's total petroleum products at current levels of consumption will have to be imported even if Georges Bank provides reserves meeting the most optimistic predictions. While deep-water ports at other sites in the Gulf and on the North Atlantic may help meet this need, the logistics of such a distribution pattern may eventually require new reception facilities near Boston or elsewhere along the coast. While this arrangement would concentrate VLCCs at a few selected points, the vessels transshipping the refined products will probably, in time, be too large for Boston to accommodate; the product tankers used for this purpose, while not approaching the gargantuan proportions of the VLCCs, will nonetheless tend to be in the upper range of the "handy-sized" class in order to maximize the economic benefits inherent in even incrementally larger tankers and, therefore, be beyond Boston's present handling capacity. Thus, New England may ultimately find itself in a similar, though not quite so severe, bind as was predicted earlier, since its current fleet is being scrapped; barges are unlikely to be able to meet the area's entire demand; and adequate dredging of Boston Harbor remains environmentally unacceptable and, in any case, would not relieve other navigational obstacles. A product terminal for New England, moreover, might ultimately prove desirable for its economic as well as supply advantages, since it would offer significant savings in petroleum transportation costs in either transshipment from domestic sources or direct shipment from foreign sources.

If an offshore terminal, either product or crude, becomes a requisite for New England's future energy supply, there is the danger that Boston may once again hold up the rear of technological progress. Several development plans have been proposed for Maine and New Hampshire, and, although groups in both areas have posed serious environmental opposition, they could eventually deprive Boston of its primary role in regional petroleum distribution. Locating an offshore facility elsewhere in New England would not realize optimum economic benefits for the region, in particular for Massachusetts, since such a siting would necessitate a high cost distribution system entailing an environmentally undesirable increase in the coastal traffic of tankers and oceangoing barges. Within the restricted range of choice available, Massport's proposed terminal site for Outer Boston Harbor appears the most favorable for Massachusetts. The Port of Boston, strategically located as the sea access of the eastern Massachusetts population concentration, is the most logical and viable site for the terminus and distribution center of a modernized energy transport system.

If Massport is ever to revive its campaign, even for just a product terminal, it will have to rectify the major deficiency in its earlier proposal and develop a comprehensive well-integrated energy plan for the entire New England region in cooperation with all interested parties, both public and private. Regional planning must be an absolute prerequisite for any project involving the critical issue of energy supply and entailing serious economic and environmental impacts. Massport must swallow the bitter pill of externalizing any future plans and operations and must be required to cooperate and coordinate with both local and regional government agencies and private interest groups. The Deepwater Port Act of 1974 itself requires a good deal of regional coordination to ensure the consistency of the states' environmental plans. Any Massport proposal would also better serve the public interest if it advocated that the facility, operated by the Port Authority, would be owned by a public corporation with a regional pipeline distribution system constructed, owned and controlled by all the participating New England states. The Deepwater Port Act actually promotes this sort of arrangement by giving priority to proposals from coastal states themselves, or combinations of states, and public corporations when there are two or more applicants for the same area at once. The public interest could be even further served if any agreement with an oil company to establish a refinery provided for the public having a voice in determining what types of petroleum products would be produced. Massport might resent this direct intrusion of the public interest into its quasi-corporate dealings, but new approaches are indicated if and when it proves necessary or desirable to develop a new energy supply and distribution system for New England.

The second horizon for the Port of Boston is that of containerization. This miracle of fast and convenient cargo transportation, along with the jet plane, improved overseas communication services, and expanding multinational commerical interests, is rapidly forging a global economy. Viewed with maximum optimism, containerization may offer Boston its first opportunity in decades to reassume the role of an important world port. On the other hand, a more pessimistic assessment would have to recognize that the belated and faltering introduction of containerization along with Boston's reputation for operational difficulties might prove recent investments futile in the face of earlier and more concentrated developments elsewhere. It is generally accepted that the North Atlantic container routes will be saturated by 1975 and that, by 1980, all additional major container trade routes will have been established. Within this time frame, expeditious execution may be the decisive factor in determining Boston's future; time has been lost in adopting the new technology and short time is left to secure a significant participation for the Port in the global web of the intermodal transportation system.

While Boston has experienced consistent and impressive success with containerization since the opening of the Moran Terminal in 1971, the future growth of the container business is not entirely assured. A number of factors contribute to this uncertainty and many of them are beyond the influence or control of the Port itself. While 1975 was a banner year for Boston, this might have been due in part to the fact that it was an unstable year for the container trade in general, and companies were seeking business wherever they could find it. A major consideration is that, if the container market stabilizes, Boston may be bypassed once again and container activities will be concentrated in larger ports generating greater volumes of trade. The increased concentration of the container trade in other North Atlantic ports remains the greatest obstacle to Boston's regeneration. This concentration is following the familiar pattern in New York, which many lines are attempting to establish as the one regional port to service all their North Atlantic traffic. An equally important antagonist for Boston in the arena of containerization is Baltimore, a dynamic port that rapidly adopted the new technology, has willingly made huge capital investments in the most advanced facilities available, and has pursued an extensive and effective solicitation campaign. Not handicapped with the congestion already experienced in New York, Baltimore has made great progress in establishing itself as a major service port for the voluminous trade of the Midwest hinterland, to which it enjoys closest proximity. As this trade becomes more and more containerized, Baltimore will more and more consolidate its position as a major container port. Furthermore, recent increases in the cost of Middle East oil have forced bunker fuel prices in some areas up to four or five times the previous levels. This, in turn, is forcing steamship lines, because of basic fuel economics, to slow their transit speed to reduce fuel consumption and call on only one port, if possible, or at least a minimum number of ports in each region. This situation has already cost Boston the service of many tramp vessels and might also curtail container ship arrivals. The increased operating costs of the larger container ships also make the labor delays common in Boston even more intolerable. Thus, another impulse towards concentration seems to be working against Boston.

Shipping in Boston, even more so than in other ports, is also facing serious and increasing competition from air carriers. The trend towards air freight, despite its expense, is based on its obvious advantages when seaborne transportation gets mired in high handling costs, pilferage, damage problems, or en route delays. The recent introduction of Lower Deck Containers carried in the bellies of new wide-body passenger jets and the increasing use of all-cargo jumbo jets will siphon even more business away from steamships and, in particular, container ships. It has been projected that, by 1980, 15 percent of all liner cargo will be carried by air.[2] These developments are ironic and especially ominous for the Boston seaport because of the convenient location and excellent services of Logan International Airport and the availability of many local high-value-low-bulk manufactures that are ideally suited for air transport, by which freight rates are generally calculated by volume rather than weight. Indicative of this situation is that, in 1974, Logan handled over 345 million pounds of cargo.

The two major problems for containerization in Boston, however, involve railroads rather than airplanes. The North American land bridge, or more properly, minibridge, really began to have an impact in early 1972. Under this system, containerized cargo arrives at an Atlantic or Pacific Coast port and is then transshipped by railroad to a consignee in a port area on the opposite coast or the Gulf of Mexico; for exports, the process works in reverse. Although the cost of such transport is slightly higher than an all-water route, the minibridge has already become an integral part of the worldwide distribution pattern of manufactured goods because it drastically reduces total transit time. Intercoastal railroad carriage requires only seven days, or one-half of the time required for waterborne carriage via the Panama Canal. While the minibridge theoretically could work in favor of ports on both coasts, the actual volume of business from Europe to the West Coast is insignificant compared to that from the Far East to the East Coast and Gulf area. Although the minibridge makes eminent sense in the light of commercial transportation economics and the railroads argue that they can only survive with its traffic, opposition to the system has been intense among Atlantic and Gulf Coast ports. This is understandable since the development of minibridge traffic has diverted cargoes from ocean carriers and ports, including Boston. It has been estimated that the minibridge from the Far East cost Boston 72,000 tons of containerized cargo in 1973, and has significantly contributed to the drop in steamship lines calling on the Port. Boston has joined with all other ports on the East and Gulf coasts in fighting the minibridge and in petitioning the Federal Maritime Commission to declare that they are illegally being deprived of cargoes. Although the minibridge offers considerable advantages in overall distribution, it can only reduce Boston's potential container business. If it continues to develop, as it probably will without a FMC ruling to the contrary, Boston will continue to suffer.

The other major problem regarding railroads for Boston will require aggressive rather than defensive efforts. If the Port is to realize its full potential in the container trade, it must exploit the inherent advantages that railroads have over trucks for long-haul container carriage. In 1973, the Boston & Maine handled over 6500 containers, of which less than a thousand were shipped through Boston and then only when the primary ports of Halifax and St. John's suffered emergency conditions such as overflows or work stoppages. In the future, when the Canadian ports reach their capacity for containers from the Midwest, the railroad plans to absorb the cost of a regular ocean "feeder line" to carry the excess volume to Boston for overseas departure. Boston must avail itself more directly and extensively of the greater carrying capacity and lower costs of rail service from the Midwest, as Baltimore has so effectively done by employing trailer-on-flatcar (TOFC) and container-on-flatcar (COFC) operations. While railroads have their greatest advantages over trucks for long hauls, the Boston & Maine feels that Boston could even compete with New York for short hauls, despite the $25 to $30 rate differential, because of the long waiting time and delays that beset the larger port. To realize any significant increase in either long- or short-haul rail business, the Moran Terminal must have improved rail facilities and an expanded consolidation service, and the Port must make better use of the available railroad systems.

The most important obstacle to Boston's increasing its share of the critical Midwest container business, however, is the present rail rate structure. Baltimore, New York, and Norfolk all enjoy more favorable rates for container traffic from the Midwest than Boston; Baltimore, with the shortest distance to the hinterland, has the lowest inland rates of all and has consequently outstripped Boston in container business. Boston currently has only one shipper concentrating solely on the Midwest and this minimal effort has produced only a trickle of containers. If the Port is to have any real chance of getting significant container business from the interior, the Federal Maritime Commission and the Interstate Commerce Commission must recognize a through bill of lading from Chicago to Antwerp and equalize intermodal rates. This predicament, dependent on external decision making, only adds to the uncertainty of future expansion of Boston's container business.

Against this background, Massport's proposed $40 million second public container terminal poses another dilemma. Though projections based on prevailing trends indicate a need for additional facilities, there is the risk that further investments might not result in any appreciable expansion of Boston's container trade. If further conditions, both within and beyond local control, do not develop in the Port's favor and if the concentration in New York and Baltimore accelerates, a second major terminal might loom as a much unneeded waterfront white elephant. On the other hand, if containerization is truly a rare opportunity for Boston to better itself, a heavy financial commitment might be well advised to better prepare the Port for its continued renaissance. There are just as many positive signs pointing in this latter direction as there are complications, and all port interests are united in their confidence that Boston can anticipate a growing and assured container market.

There is ample evidence that containerization has been the first genuinely encouraging development in the Port of Boston for many years. The volume of container trade has quickly surpassed predictions and has had a generally rejuvenative effect on port activity and morale. Investments in the Moran Terminal, though they could have been earlier and better planned, so far have paid off handsomely; despite losing 38 strike days, 1974 was the best year yet for the Port. Containerization has offered Massport a bonafide waterfront cause, and it has responded with an aggressive policy on port development that promises to continue. Moreover, as the heyday of general air transportation passes and the master plan for Logan Airport nears completion, port programs may become more feasible than ever; after consistent increases for many years, commercial air operations at Logan dropped in 1974 due to the introduction of wide-bodied jets, consolidation of flights, and the slackening in the economy. All indications are that air facilities will no longer demand the intense expansion efforts that they have in the past and thus, in turn, will offer a significant opportunity to switch investment patterns and spotlight port development.

Most importantly, a broad political and economic consensus has crystallized in favor of increased containerization of the Port of Boston. A special task force established by the mayor of Boston has restudied harbor facilities and come out in strong support of expanding the Moran Terminal and developing a second major container facility on the site of the South Boston Naval Annex.[3] The unanimous backing of the twenty-man coalition of business and government executives, including such key personalities as the state Transportation Secretary, the director of the Boston Redevelopment Authority, and the chairman of the First National Bank of Boston, indicates the possibility for a unified, cooperative, and coordinated approach to port improvement that has been lacking in the past. Although the coalition's proposal is only advisory, because its members represent considerable power, it adds a major thrust to the campaign for expanded containerization. In the end, Boston seems to have balanced the future uncertainties against the prospective gains and decided confidently to follow through its commitment to containerization.

Whatever final decisions are made on the future of containerization in Boston, the local waterfront labor situation will be a crucial factor in any further port modernization. Continued labor problems will at least make efficient operation and orderly development more difficult and might even force many of the hard-won container lines to abandon the Port. Labor faces a dilemma unsettling to its customary pursuit of its own self-interests. It has been forced to recognize that the survival of shipping in Boston requires that organized labor cooperate with efforts at modernization, the very process that ironically dictates a decimation of its own ranks. Labor has had to accept a demoralizing reduction in the manhours needed in the Port from 1.7 million in 1969 to an estimated 900,000 in 1974. Management, too, has had to make a difficult adjustment in recognizing that, in return for modernization, labor has an intrinsic right to either a guaranteed employment level or commensurate compensation. The Port is fortunate that the intractable "closed shop" union practice is allowing a natural attrition of the labor roles, but this unplanned mechanism for self-adjustment doesn't really ease tensions between labor and management in the short run. The Port's factional disputes are exacerbated by the relative lack of union leadership since the demise of John F. Moran and the continuation of New York's influence and control. Moreover, Boston's waterfront labor tends to become embroiled over local issues, such as the flexibility of work rules, much more readily and persistently than workers at other North Atlantic ports.

All of these factors prompted uneasy predictions that a damaging general strike would ensue when the existing labor contract ran out at the end of September 1974. Unfortunately for all port interests, these predictions were realized. In July 1974, Boston longshoremen had ratified the new three-year master contract for North Atlantic ports that had been negotiated in New York. This national contract established new wage scales, setting longshoremen's wages at $6.80 an hour on September 30, 1974, with two annual increments amounting to $8.00 an hour by September 30, 1976. For five months however, although the payscale was not at issue, negotiations failed to resolve local contract terms; Boston was the only North Atlantic port not to reach local agreement. On December 8, the four major locals rejected the final contract offer from the Boston Shipping Association and began the first general waterfront strike since the fall of 1971. Although there was disagreement over hours of employment and the reduction of gang size in recent years, the major precipitating issue was a guaranteed annual income.

The local union demanded a guaranteed annual income based on 2080 hours of work per year, the same level prevailing in New York and previously provided for in Boston's most recent contract. The BSA, on the other hand, insisted on a reduction to 1000 guaranteed annual hours and felt this was a fair offer since, based on the new wage scale, it constituted an increase of $1.5 million over the three-year contract period. Both labor and management offered the classic arguments in support of their positions, arguments firmly rooted in the quandry of port modernization when labor-intensive practices confront capital-intensive technology. Labor, understandably defensive, claimed that only 25 percent of the 1100 strikers had been working regularly. Although they realized they would never again be needed in great numbers, the longshoremen recognized the crucial role they played in port operations and felt they were justified in protecting their immediate interests; their very availability demanded that, if actual work could not be provided, then a commensurate guaranteed income was a necessity. The BSA, for its part, felt that 2080 guaranteed work hours was an unrealistic level of compensation and one Boston could no longer afford. The Port's longshoremen were anticipated to work only 500,000 total actual manhours in 1975, compared to 1.5 million in 1970, and the BSA believed this gap made it impossible to maintain such a high degree of guaranteed income. Arthur Lane, President of the BSA, argued that, while New York could afford 2080 hours, this demand was incompatible with conditions in Boston and would have disastrous results: "There is not enough business in Boston to once again support a guaranteed annual wage of 2080 hours. All that would do is to make Boston noncompetitive with other ports because we would have to raise our operating costs, which are paid by visiting vessels."[4]

Though both labor and management remained intransigent, both sides realized the difficulty of the situation and the real danger of losing lines and business. BSA President Lane saw the strike as potentially the most damaging in the Port's history because Boston was completely isolated: "None of them [other north Atlantic ports] are striking, and places like Portland, Maine and New York City are waiting outside our door for business."[5] For the same reasons, ILA Vice President Edward Dalton recognized that, in the long run, the strike would hurt Boston longshoremen more than the BSA. Yet neither side could offer any resolution to the predicament.

To make matters worse, on December 12, the ILA declined even to meet with the BSA unless the 70¢ per hour raise in the master contract was made retroactive to October 1. The BSA refused, arguing that their position was consistent with the understanding reached by the Council of North Atlantic Shipping Associations during the master contract negotiations. The situation had reached such an impasse that ILA President Thomas Gleason journeyed from New York to enter local contract talks for the first time since 1968. Once again, New York's influence was decisive and Gleason's direct intervention soon broke the deadlock. On December 20, Boston dock workers voted to end the strike and 900 longshoremen returned to work under the terms of the old contract until agreement is reached on a new pact. The BSA, meanwhile, is preparing a study on comparative costs at East Coast ports to present to Boston labor, but some observers feel this will not have any persuasive impact.

Whatever final outcome emerges from Boston's latest labor-management conflict, it most likely will be as fragile as those of the past. Stable labor conditions remain a key to present operations and future progress. There is a glaring need for an improved labor situation that would prevent or at least minimize self-defeating tactics, break down barriers between conflicting port segments, and develop a more unified port structure. Energies traditionally consumed by often petty and debilitative differences could more readily be focused into constructive channels. Improvements must be made if Boston is to present the much more salable posture of a dynamic, consolidated port with a promising future before it. A new approach is indicated since the old approach has failed to produce the labor stability that the Port so desperately needs.

Presently aggravating all Port difficulties, including the labor situation, is the fact that the Massachusetts Port Authority, the focal point of all waterfront activity, is in the most precarious position since its establishment. In November 1974, by a four to three vote the Port Authority Board, led by Chairman James A. Fay, requested Edward King to resign after serving as Executive Director for eleven years. Although King at first vowed to fight his dismissal on technicalities stemming from the absence of any formal list of complaints, before long he acquiesced in the board's request, influenced at least in part by a generous $100,000 settlement in severance pay and accrued vacation benefits.

King's dismissal kicked up a political storm of controversy, but this was instigated less by the firing itself than by the unseemly manner in which it was done. The whole unpleasant affair had the unnecessary air of a palace coup with intimations of behind the scenes plotting between board members and the governor's office. Although neither Governor Sargent, who had just been defeated in his bid for reelection, nor Governor-elect Michael Dukakis were supporters of King's mode of administering the Port Authority and were both accused of involvement in his ouster, at most, they appear to have adopted a hands-off policy. King himself absolved both of any implication in his firing and admitted it was a difference in philosophy between himself and some board members that was at the root of the problem.

King was accurate in his assessment since, beneath it all, it was simply a difference in philosophical approaches that inevitably brought Fay and the executive director to odds over Massport's master planning, particularly at Logan Airport, with King continuing to promote expansion and Fay espousing an approach more integrated with other transportation requirements. At the crux of the matter, of course, was the long-running conflict, revolving around the airport, over the proper interpretation of the public interest; while King's programs and style had an invigorating effect on the business community, they had a devastating impact on the communities surrounding Logan Airport.

This dichotomy is reflected in public statements surrounding King's dismissal. William J. McCarthy, powerful counsel for the Associated Industries of Massachusetts, faithfully represented the opinion of businessmen and many political leaders when he lauded King's accomplishments:

He has become one of the few men in Massachusetts who approached the ideal of undispensability in state government. Industry in this state came to regard Massport under his leadership as a model of efficiency in a maze of bureaucratic inefficiency and an economic jewel in an otherwise sick economy.[6]

While most commercial interests were apprehensive about the adverse effects King's dismissal would have on both the Port Authority and the general economic climate of the region, people on the opposite side of the fence seemed thoroughly gratified and relieved. John Vitagliano, Manager of the Little City

Hall in East Boston, the area hardest hit by airport expansion, aptly summarized the antagonism towards King that had festered for so long:

King made the people feel like they had no voice at all in determining their own future. From the community standpoint, the impact of King was all negative. In all controversies, he showed no flexibility or alternative.[7]

However manifested, the basic incompatibility was between King's approach, which had been necessary and magnificently productive in an earlier day, and the values of a new era:

Behind the move to oust King lies a philosophy more oriented toward the community and the environment than the economy and the Authority's profit. The philosophy is concerned with limiting automobile and airplane traffic at Logan Airport and with overall state transportation planning.[8]

This basic philosophical conflict had not been entirely resolved by King's departure nor will it be automatically resolved by a replacement more in line with the attitudes of the Port Authority Board. The issue remains of what the Commonwealth of Massachusetts, not the Massport Board or Executive Director, perceives the public interest to be and how it wants its transportation system to serve that interest. To this end, a number of legislative proposals have been submitted for the reorganization of the Port Authority, including a bill that would replace the post of executive director and abolish the seven-man board of directors. The most important factor in reassessing the orientation of the Port Authority will certainly be the attitude of Governor Dukakis, an aggressive executive who promises to exercise a good deal of political independence. Dukakis has long been convinced that Massport has to be more sensitive to community needs and the requirements for more balanced means of transportation. While believing that Massport's managerial and administrative independence ought to be preserved, he feels board appointees should be more responsive to the governor and that the governor should determine policies along with board members. Dukakis has stated that he will seek to reduce the independence of the Authority and that he would consider supporting legislation to restructure the Authority, creating a single administrator responsible to him and possibly eliminating the board altogether.

Undoubtedly, Massport should and will be more integrated into the state government structure and overall transportation planning and more conscious of communities and the environment. While the expansion of Logan Airport precipitated this redirection, it will of course have an impact on seaport development, although the two enterprises present distinctly different situations. If the reorganization of the Port Authority means an across-the-board dampening of development, the sins of the airport will in effect be visited upon the seaport and there will be the danger of diluting Boston's chances to consolidate its maritime gains and exploit whatever potential lies ahead. Already, the morale at Massport's Maritime Division has suffered and key personnel have departed. Seaport development does not have to be so contentious as airport development, but it will require some of the aggressive attention accorded Logan in the past. If Massport is to be rearranged, it would seem prudent and appropriate to assure it the resources and flexibility necessary for a continued action program in the Port, with due regard to community interests and a comprehensive transportation plan. Massport should be allowed to exercise, albeit with discretion and a clearer and coordinated conception of the public interest, adequate advocacy powers for further port development.

Furthermore, until port operations have established their profitability, Massport may require some outside financial assistance for increased port expansion, as is the case with other North Atlantic port agencies. Acting Executive Director Edward Hanley has already indicated that combined port revenues are not yet adequate to support major new investments and that a second container terminal at the South Boston Naval Annex would be possible only with some public subsidy.[9] Some such arrangement will be all the more necessary if King's dismissal and a reorganization of the Authority affect the agency's future borrowing power. Increased assistance for port development need not be exclusively financial, however. If Massport's autonomy is restrained, as it properly should be, the Port Authority will require more direct support from state government leaders in its efforts to revitalize the Port. Partly by its own design and partly by government indifference, Massport has often had to pursue the Port's cause in outside arenas without the interest or support of Massachusetts' political leaders. While other states have usually closed ranks behind their port agencies when confronting external decision-making processes, especially within the federal government, Massport has not enjoyed such mobilized backing. Its efforts on behalf of the Port would be greatly enhanced if the state, while clipping Massport's wings with one hand, offered such assistance with the other. History and recent events have demonstrated how external factors can have a critical impact on maritime activities in Boston. While these factors are usually beyond any local control, in some cases they can be judiciously and properly influenced to the decided advantages of the Port of Boston.

The Port of Boston could also benefit greatly from a less direct but nonetheless invaluable change in its relations with Massachusetts as a whole. Any campaign to restore Boston's maritime importance would stand a much better chance if the general public displayed more interest in the Port and was better informed about its past and future development. The public relations study cited in an earlier chapter discovered through polls that, among the total state population, the bulk of criticism aimed at the Port Authority was concerned with the alledged decline of the Boston seaport. Unfortunately, the majority of the populace is sadly ill-informed about port activities and the significant achievements realized in recent years that truly do serve the public interest. The Commonwealth as a whole, along with all port interests, would decidedly benefit from a concerned and comprehensively and accurately informed general public that could appreciate the seaport's long struggle and the admirable efforts being expended for its much hoped for revival. It would be to everyone's advantage if unfounded criticism were minimized and a civic pride materialized that would foster a more encouraging climate for optimum port development.

In conclusion, the Port of Boston has been almost tragically beset by a confluence of dilemmas that most ports only experience partially at any one time. There has been no miracle, not even that of containerization, that has yet been able to completely lift this persistent burden. Such technological developments, however, offer the Port a range of choices not previously available. The Port, as any functional unit, may endure them without full exploitation or apply ingenuity and effort to advance on their crest. Subsequent decisions will be crucial. Nevertheless, the Port has exhibited a stubborn courage that, in the end, gained valuable time and may allow the evolution of answers to some of its compounded problems. If not, its demise would be felt only in the Commonwealth, or at most in New England, with little impact on the national seaborne trade. Yet its history would seem to demand its survival if only as a regional outport. Be that as it may, the Port of Boston has recently made progress, though its management, labor force, and shipping concerns are not free of justified criticism, and may truly be better prepared to resolve its dilemmas and regain its stature as a respected center of maritime commerce.

**Notes**

## Chapter 1
## The History of the Port

1. Bernard Bailyn and Lotte Bailyn, *Massachusetts Shipping 1697-1714, A Statistical Study* (Cambridge: The Belknap Press of Harvard University Press, 1959), table II, p. 79.

2. Ibid., p. 22.

3. Ibid., p. 39.

4. Workers of the Writers' Program of the Work Projects Administration, *Boston Looks Seaward, The Story of the Port, 1630-1940* (Boston: Bruce Humphries, 1941), p. 55.

5. Ibid., pp. 55, 56.

6. Bailyn, op. cit., table XIII, p. 97.

7. Ibid., table XVII, p. 105.

8. Ibid., table XV, p. 99.

9. Ibid., p. 74.

10. Ibid., p. 56.

11. Robert Greenhalgh Albion with Jennie Barnes Pope, *The Rise of the Port of New York, 1815-1860* (New York: Scribner, 1939), p. 4.

12. Ibid., p. 5.

13. Samuel Eliot Morison, *The Maritime History of Massachusetts, 1783-1860* (Boston: Houghton Mifflin, 1921), p. 215. (Sentry Edition, 1961, p. 192.)

14. Ibid., p. 215.

15. Albion, op. cit., pp. 12-15.

16. Ibid., p. 46.

17. Morison, op. cit., p. 213.

18. Writers' Program, op. cit., p. 112.

19. Ibid.

20. Ibid.

21. Secretary of the Treasury, *Commerce and Navigation Reports* (Washington, D.C.: 1857).

22. Boston Board of Trade, *Fourth Annual Report* (Boston: 1858), p. 85.

23. Morison, op. cit., pp. 369, 370.

24. Edwin J. Clapp, *The Port of Boston, A Study and a Solution of the Traffic and Operating Problems of Boston, and its place in the Competition of the North Atlantic Seaports* (New Haven: Yale University Press, 1916), p. 4.

25. Writers' Program, op. cit., p. 161.

26. Ibid., p. 178.

27. U.S. Army Corps of Engineers, *Waterborne Commerce of the United States, Calendar Year 1929,* part 1 (Washington D.C.: Department of the Army, 1930).

28. Ibid.

29. Writers' Program, op. cit., pp. 213, 214.

30. Clapp, op. cit., pp. 40–41.

31. Ibid., p. 87.

32. Ibid., p. 88.

33. *Report of the Special Commission Relative to the Boston Port Authority and the Promotion and Development of the Port of Boston,* Massachusetts Legislative Documents: House, 1938, no. 209, p. 38.

34. U.S. Army Corps of Engineers, op. cit: and U.S. Army Corps of Engieers, *Waterborne Commerce of the United States, Calendar Year 1932* (Washington, D.C.: Department of the Army, 1933).

35. Clapp, op. cit., p. 20.

36. Ibid.

37. U.S. Army Corps of Engineers, *Waterborne Commerce of the United States, Calendar Year 1972* (Washington, D.C.: Department of the Army, 1973).

**Chapter 2**
**Administration of the Port**

1. *An Act to Create Boards of Harbor and Land Commissioners,* Chapter 149 of the Massachusetts Acts and Resolves of 1877.

2. *An Act to Create a Board of Harbor and Land Commissioners,* Chapter 263 of the Massachusetts Acts and Resolves of 1879.

3. *An Act to Purchase Land in East Boston,* Chapter 648 of the Massachusetts Acts and Resolves of 1910.

4. *An Act Relative to the Development of the Port of Boston,* Chapter 748 of the Massachusetts Acts and Resolves of 1911.

5. Ibid., p. 991.

6. *An Act Relative to the Directors of the Port of Boston,* Chapter 712 of the Massachusetts Acts and Resolves of 1914.

7. Directors of the Port of Boston, *Port of Boston USA* (Boston: 1915), p. 1.

8. *An Act to Create a Commission on Waterways and Public Lands,* Chapter 288 of the Massachusetts Acts and Resolves of 1916.

9. *An Act to Organize in Departments the Executive and Administrative Functions of the Commonwealth,* Chapter 350 of the Acts and Resolves of 1919.

10. *Report of the Special Commission Relative to the Boston Port Authority and the Promotion and Development of the Port of Boston,* Massachusetts Legislative Documents: House, 1938, no. 29, p. 14.

11. *An Act Establishing the Boston Port Authority,* Chapter 229 of the Massachusetts Acts and Resolves of 1929.

12. Ibid., p. 239.

13. U.S. Army Corps of Engineers, *Waterborne Commerce of the United States, Calendar Year 1972*, part 1 (Washington, D.C.: Department of the Army, 1973).

14. *Report of the Special Commission*, 1938, op. cit., p. 18.

15. *Special Report of the Boston Port Authority Relative to the Causes for Withdrawal of Shipping Business From the Port of Boston and to Wharfage Charges at Said Port*, Massachusetts Legislative Documents, House, 1943, vol. 4, no. 1273, p. 6.

16. *An Act Abolishing the Boston Port Authority, and Establishing a Port of Boston Authority*, Chapter 619 of the Massachusetts Acts and Resolves of 1945.

17. *Report of the Special Commission Relative to the Rights, Powers and Duties of the Port of Boston Authority*, Massachusetts Legislative Documents: Senate, 1950, vol. 2, no. 655, p. 12.

18. *An Act Abolishing the Port of Boston Authority and Establishing the Port of Boston Commission*, Chapter 608 of the Massachusetts Acts and Resolves of 1953.

19. *Report of the Special Commission on the Massachusetts Port Authority*, Massachusetts Legislative Documents: House, 1956, vol. 3, no. 2575, p. 15.

20. Walter P. Hedden, *Mission: Port Development* (Washington, D.C.: American Association of Port Authorities, 1967), p. 76.

21. *Report of the Special Commission*, 1956, op. cit., p. 12.

22. Ibid., p. 95.

23. *Report of the Governor's Revenue Authority Advisory Committee*, Massachusetts Legislative Documents: House, 1955, vol. 8, no. 2983, p. 40.

24. *Report of the Special Commission*, 1956, op. cit., p. 37.

25. *An Act Establishing the Massachusetts Port Authority*, Chapter 465 of the Massachusetts Acts and Resolves of 1956, p. 2.

26. *Senate Requested Supreme Judicial Court Opinion on the Bill to Create the Massachusetts Port Authority*, Massachusetts Legislative Documents: Senate, 1956, vol. 2, no. 704, p. 20.

27. Ibid., p. 25.

## Chapter 3
The Constitution of the Port: Trade Imbalance and Petroleum

1. Samuel A. Lawrence, *International Sea Transport: The Years Ahead* (Lexington, Mass.: Lexington Books, D.C. Heath and Co., 1972), p. 64.

2. "Boston Hasn't Halted Its Shipping Decline," *Christian Science Monitor,* March 31, 1967, p. 2.

3. Abt Associates, Inc., *The Boston Seaport, 1970–1990* (Cambridge: Abt Associates, Inc., 1970), p. 21.

4. Rowland and MacNeal, *Port of Boston Waterborne Commerce Market and Development Requirements*, (New York, 1964), chapter 5, p. 12.

5. "New Cargoes for Boston Harbor," *Christian Science Monitor*, May 6, 1967, p. 2.

6. Ibid.

7. "Boston Expected to Continue Container and Cruise Gains," *Boston Globe*, January 13, 1974, p. A-10.

8. Legislative Research Council, *Report Relative to the Promotion of the Port of Boston*, Massachusetts Legislative Documents: House, 1968, vol. 10, no. 4852.

9. *Equalization of Rates of North Atlantic Ports*, 311 Interstate Commerce Commission 689 (1959).

10. *Boston & Maine Railroad* v. *U.S.*, 202F, supp. 830 (1962).

11. *Baltimore & Ohio Railroad* v. *Boston & Maine Railroad*, 373 U.S. 372 (1963).

12. "Rates Verdict to Spur Port, New England Railroads," *Boston Globe,* May 21, 1963, p. 13. Courtesy of the Boston Globe.

13. Ibid.

14. Ibid.

15. "Bins Closed—Boston Loses Grain Deal," *Boston Globe*, February 10, 1966, p. 3.

16. *Massachusetts Port Authority Annual Report,* 1964, p. 10.

17. *MPA Annual Report*, 1962, p. 19.

18. U.S. Department of Transportation, *St. Lawrence Seaway Development Corporation 1972 Annual Report* (Washington, D.C.: U.S. Government Printing Office, 1973). p. 18.

19. Ibid., p. 9.

20. *1968 Legislative Report*, p. 59.

21. Wallace P. Sansone, "Domestic Shipping and American Maritime Policy," *U.S. Naval Institute Proceedings, Naval Review 1974*, pp. 176–177.

22. Abt Associates, Inc., *The Boston Seaport, 1970–1990* (Cambridge Abt Associates, Inc., 1970), p. 21.

23. Ibid., pp. 42, 152.

24. U.S. Army Corps of Engineers, *Waterborne Commerce of the United States, Calendar Year 1972*, part 1 (Washington, D.C.: Department of the Army, 1973).

25. Frederic R. Harris, Inc., *Feasibility Investigation: Massport Out-To-Sea Oil Terminal System, Interim Report,* Boston, 1970, p. 21.

26. Abt Associates, Inc., op. cit., pp. 98, 99.

27. Ibid., p. 168.

28. U.S. Department of Commerce, Maritime Administration, *Draft Environmental Impact Statement, Tanker Program* (Washington, D.C.: U.S. Government Printing Office, 1973), sec. IV, p. 198.

29. Edwin M. Hood, *Statement Before Committee on Merchant Marine and Fisheries, House of Representatives*, July 11, 1973, p. 2.

30. U.S. Department of Commerce, Maritime Administration, *Draft Environmental Impact Statement, Tanker Program* (Washington, D.C.: U.S. Government Printing Office, 1973), sec. IV, p. 198.

31. Massachusetts Institute of Technology, *Economic Factors in the Development of a Coastal Zone* (Cambridge: M.I.T. Press, 1970).

32. Harris, op. cit.

33. E. H. Harlow, Senior Vice President, Frederic R. Harris, Inc., to Edward J. King, Massport Executive Director, March 6, 1970, "Letter of Transmittal," Feasibility Investigation: Massport Out-To-Sea Oil Terminal System, Interim Report, (Boston, 1970).

34. Harris, op. cit., p. 11.

35. Ibid., p. 7.

36. Ibid., p. 69.

37. Harris, *"Letter of Transmittal,"* op. cit.

38. "Massport's oil project labelled contradictory by State Sen. Bulger," *Boston Globe*, October 6, 1972, p. 3.

39. Ibid. Courtesy of the Boston Globe.

40. MarAd, *Tanker Program*, sec. IV, p. 4.

41. Joseph Kasputys and Joe Bill Young, "Subsidies, Seed Money, and National Security," *Seapower* (September 1973), p. 24.

42. MarAd, *Tanker Program*, op. cit., sec. IV, p. 203.

43. U.S. Department of Commerce, Maritime Administration, *MARAD 1970: Year of Transition, Annual Report for Fiscal Year 1970* (Washington, D.C.: U.S. Government Printing Office, 1971), appendix II, pp. 62, 64.

44. MarAd, *Tanker Program*, op. cit., sec. VI, p. 49.

45. "U.S. Shipbuilding Report," *Marine Engineering/Log* (February 1974), pp. 72, 74.

46. Ibid.

47. U.S. Department of Commerce, Maritime Administration, *Pending Construction Differential Subsidy Applications* (Washington, D.C.: U.S. Government Printing Office, 1973).

48. Hood, op. cit., p. 4.

49. President Nixon's Energy Message to the U.S. Congress, April 18, 1973.

50. MarAd, *Tanker Program*, op. cit., sec. IV, p. 203.

51. U.S. Congress, House, Committee on Merchant Marine and Fisheries, *High Seas Oil Port Act,* Report 93-692 to Accompany H.R. 5898, 93rd Congress, 1st Session, 1973, p. 15.

52. Frederic R. Harris, Inc., *Feasibility Investigation: Massport Out-To-Sea Oil Terminal, Supplemental Report,* Boston, 1971, p. 3.

53. *Massachusetts Port Authority 1972 Annual Report*, p. 7.

54. MARAD, *Tanker Program*, op. cit., sec. IX, p. 2.

55. U.S. Congress, House, *Offshore Ports and Terminals, Hearing before the House Committee on Merchant Marine and Fisheries on H.R. 5090 and H.R. 5898,* 93rd Congress, 1st Session, 1973, p. 142.

56. U.S. Department of Commerce, Maritime Administration, *Draft Environmental Impact Statement, Tanker Program* (Washington, D.C.: U.S. Government Printing Office, 1973, sec. IV, p. 43.

57. "New England's Dilemma," *Time*, April 22, 1974, p. 50.

58. William E. Shoupp, *World Energy and the Oceans*, Second Annual Sea Grant Lecture, (Massachusetts Institute of Technology, Sea Grant Program: Report No. MITSG 74-7, 1973).

59. Wallace P. Sansone, "Domestic Shipping and American Maritime Policy," U.S. Naval Institute Proceedings, Naval Review, 1974.

60. "King Presses for Offshore Oil Terminal," *Boston Herald American*, November 12, 1973, p. 3.

61. "Bay State Congressmen Back Massport Oil Terminal," *Boston Globe*, November 11, 1973, p. 17.

62. "Winthrop Oil Terminal Plan Gets Morale Boost, $500,000 for Study," *Boston Globe*, September 22, 1973, p. 16.

63. "New England Public Oil Corporation Urged," *Christian Science Monitor,* December 5, 1973, p. 3.

64. "Anatomy of a Fiasco," *Boston Herald American*, January 9, 1974, p. 1.

## Chapter 4
## Constitution of the Port: Port Facilities and Cost Structure

1. Arthur D. Little, Inc., *North Atlantic Port Survey: Report to the Boston Shipping Association*, Cambridge, 1966, p. 19.

2. *1968 Legislative Report*, p. 45.

3. Abt Associates, Inc., *The Boston Seaport, 1970–1990* (Cambridge: Abt Associates, Inc., 1970), p. 98.

4. Abe Plotkin, "The Port and Parity: How Boston Got the 'Business'," *Boston*, vol. 55, no. 8, (September 1963), pp. 50–61.

5. "BSA Charges Fly," *Boston Globe*, February 10, 1966, p. 3.

6. *Massachusetts Port Authority 1967 Annual Report.*

7. Arthur D. Little, op. cit., p. 90.

8. Chester W. Hartman et al, *The Massachusetts Port Authority: Public Purpose and Public Accountability*, Cambridge, 1970, sec. II, p. 12.

9. Ibid., sec. IV, p. 5.

10. *Massachusetts Port Authority 1973 Annual Report.*

11. Anthony J. Yudes, "Airport and Labor Top Lures in Bringing Business to Boston," *Boston Evening Globe*, March 15, 1974, p. 23.

12. Federal Maritime Commission, Bureau of Domestic Regulation, Division of Terminals, *Staff Study of the Port of Boston* (Washington, D.C.: U.S. Government Printing Office, 1967), p. 46.

13. *1968 Legislative Report*, p. 22.

14. Arthur D. Little, op. cit., p. 30.

15. "Boston Shipping Association Protests MPA $1 Surcharge," *Boston Globe*, January 27, 1966, p. 5.

16. "MPA, New Role," *Boston Globe*, February 10, 1966, p. 1.

## Chapter 5
## Constitution of the Port: Labor and Competition with
## New York

1. *FMC Staff Study*, pp. 42, 44.

2. James Hammond, "Problems that Plague the Port," *Boston*, vol, 60, no. 2 (February 1968), p. 45.

3. Edward Francis, *The Truth About the Port of Boston* (Boston: City of Boston Printing Section, 1967), p. 13.

4. *1968 Legislative Report*, p. 54.

5. Massachusetts Institute of Technology, Report No. 21, *Project Bosporus, Boston Port Utilization Study* (Cambridge: M.I.T. Press, 1970), p. 16.

6. "Boston Port Decline Faces Quiz," *Christian Science Monitor*, March 28, 1967, p. 7.

7. "Containers Crucial to Boston Shipping," *Boston Globe*, July 9, 1972, p. 25. Courtesy of the Boston Globe.

8. Hammond, op. cit., p. 46.

9. *Massachusetts Port Authority 1969 Annual Report*, p. 30.

10. *Bosporus*, op. cit., p. 238.

11. *FMC Staff Study*, p. 38.

12. Chester W. Hartman et al, *The Massachusetts Port Authority: Public Purpose and Public Accountability*, Cambridge, 1970, sec. II, p. 15.

13. *Massachusetts Port Authority 1969 Annual Report*, p. 29.

14. Edward Francis, op. cit., p. 2.

15. Ibid., p. 6.

16. *FMC Staff Study*, p. 18.

Chapter 6
Constitution of the Port: Containerization and Massport

1. "Containers Crucial to Boston Shipping," *Boston Globe*, July 9, 1972, p. 25.

2. Samuel A. Lawrence, *International Sea Transport: The Years Ahead* (Lexington, Mass.: Lexington, 1972), p. 65.

3. James Hammond, "Soundings at the Port — High Tides Ahead," *Boston*, vol. 62, no. 2 (February 1970), p. 65.

4. Chester W. Hartman et al, *The Massachusetts Port Authority: Public Purpose and Public Accountability*, Cambridge, 1970, sec. II, p. 10.

5. Ibid., p. 6.

6. "Will New Container Crane Revitalize Boston's Port," *Christian Science Monitor,* June 21, 1971, p. 4. Reprinted by permission from *The Christian Science Monitor* © 1971 The Christian Science Publishing Society. All rights reserved.

7. "Containers Crucial to Boston Shipping," *Boston Globe*, July 9, 1972, p. 25.

8. Ibid.

9. U.S. Army Corps of Engineers, *Waterborne Commerce of the United States, Calendar Year 1972* (Washington, D.C.: Department of the Army, 1973).

10. Charles F. Davis, "Ship Industry Reports Inland Export Cargoes Backed Up," *Journal of Commerce* (March 6, 1974), p. 1.

11. Edward Francis, "Steamship Lines May End Land Bridge," *Boston Sunday Herald Advertiser,* March 31, 1974, p. 58.

12. "Hub to Get $30m Terminal," *Boston Sunday Herald Traveler and Advertiser*, July 2, 1972, p. 24.

13. "Containing a Port Facility," *Boston Globe,* February 28, 1974. p. 18. Courtesy of the Boston Globe.

14. Massachusetts Institute of Technology, Report No. 21, *Project Bosporus, Boston Port Utilization Study* (Cambridge: M.I.T. Press, 1970), pp. 171-172.

15. Ibid., p. 257.

16. James Hammond, "Perspective on the Port," *Boston*, vol. 59, no. 2 (February 1967), p. 54.

17. *Massachusetts Port Authority 1969 Annual Report*, p. 29.

18. Ibid., p. 29.

19. Hartman et al, op. cit., sec. I, pp. 4–5.

20. Alan Lupo, "The Monarch of Massport," *Boston*, vol. 62, no. 7 (July 1973), p. 70.

21. Hartman et al, op. cit., sec. V, p. 14.

22. Lupo, op. cit., p. 33.

23. "House kills bill giving Sargent control over Massport spending," *Boston Globe*, March 27, 1974, p. 3.

24. Andy Merton, "Why Slow-and-Steady Can't Lose in '74," *Boston*, vol. 66, no. 3 (March 1974), p. 41.

25. John A. S. McGlennon, Regional Administrator, Environmental Protection Agency, Letter to Honorable Robert H. Quinn, Attorney General, Commonwealth of Massachusetts, August 2, 1973.

26. "Massport Curb Won by White," *Boston Globe*, March 14, 1974, p. 12.

27. *An Act Establishing a Division of Environmental Protection within the Department of the Attorney General and Directing the Preparation of Environmental Impact Reports,* Chapter 781 of *Massachusetts Acts and Resolves of 1972,* p. 740.

28. Hartman et al, op. cit., sec. VI, p. 2.

29. "Boston Port Decline Faces Quiz," *Christian Science Monitor*, March 28, 1967, p. 7.

30. Newsome and Co., Inc., *Public Relations Study and Recommendations Prepared for the Massachusetts Port Authority*, Boston, 1972, sec. II, p. 3.

31. Hartman et al, op. cit., sec. IV, p. 5.

## Chapter 7
## The Future of the Port

1. "Spills Decline," *Industry* (February 1975), p. 21.

2. Samuel A. Lawrence, *International Sea Transport: The Years Ahead* (Lexington, Mass.: Lexington, 1972), p. 142.

3. "Boston Container Terminal at Naval Annex is Urged," *Boston Globe*, March 6, 1975, p. 19.

4. "Strike Isolates Boston, Shipper Says," *Boston Globe*, December 11, 1974, p. 4. Courtesy of the Boston Globe.

5. Ibid.

6. "Over the Years, Massport Has Made Friends, Enemies with Controversial Director," *Boston Globe*, November 22, 1974, p. 3.

7. Ibid.

8. "King Firing: A Month of Planning," *Boston Sunday Globe*, November 24, 1974, p. 1. Courtesy of the Boston Globe.

9. "Boston Container Terminal at Naval Annex is Urged," *Boston Globe*, March 6, 1975, p. 19.

**Bibliography**

# Bibliography

## Books

Albion, Robert G., with Pope, Jennie B. *The Rise of the Port of New York 1815–1860.* New York: Scribner, 1939.

Bailyn, Bernard and Lotte. *Massachusetts Shipping 1697 – 1714 A Statistical Study.* Cambridge, Mass.: The Belknap Press of Harvard University Press, 1959.

Branch, Alan E. *Elements of Shipping.* London: Chapman and Hall, 1964.

Clapp, Edwin J. *The Port of Boston: A Study and a Solution of the Traffic and Operating Problems of Boston, and its Place in the Competition of the North Atlantic Seaports.* New Haven: Yale University Press, 1916.

Francis, Edward. *The Truth About the Port of Boston.* Boston: City of Boston Printing Section, 1967.

Hedden, Walter P. *Mission: Port Development.* Washington, D.C.: The American Association of Port Authorities, 1967.

Kendall, Lane C. *The Business of Shipping.* Cambridge, Maryland: Cornell Maritime Press, 1973.

Lawrence, Samuel A. *International Sea Transport: The Years Ahead.* Lexington, Mass.: Lexington, 1972.

Morison, Samuel Eliot. *The Maritime History of Massachusetts 1783–1860.* Boston: Houghton Mifflin, 1921; Sentry Edition, 1961.

Oram, R. B. *Cargo Handling and the Modern Port.* London: Pergamon, 1965.

Workers of the Writers' Program of the Work Projects Administration. *Boston Looks Seaward, The Story of the Port, 1630–1940.* Boston: Bruce Humphries, 1941.

## Reports (chronological)

Secretary of the Treasury. *Commerce and Navigation Reports.* Washington, D.C.: 1857.

Boston Board of Trade. *Fourth Annual Report.* Boston: 1858.

Directors of the Port of Boston. *Port of Boston U.S.A.* Boston: 1915.

U.S. Army Corps of Engineers. *Waterborne Commerce of the United States.* Washington, D.C.: Department of the Army, 1920 - 1972.

*Report of the Special Commission Relative to the Boston Port Authority and the Promotion and Development of the Port of Boston.* Massachusetts Legislative Documents: House, 1938, no. 209.

*Special Report of the Boston Port Authority Relative to the Causes for Withdrawal of Shipping Business From the Port of Boston and to Wharfage Charges at Said Port.* Massachusetts Legislative Documents: House, 1943, vol. 4, no. 1273.

*Report of the Special Commission Relative to the Rights, Powers and Duties of the Port of Boston Authority.* Massachusetts Legislative Documents: Senate, 1950, vol. 2, no. 655.

*Report of the Governor's Revenue Authority Advisory Committee.* Massachusetts Legislative Documents: House, 1955, vol. 8, no. 2983.

*Report of the Special Commission on the Massachusetts Port Authority.* Massachusetts Legislative Documents: House, 1956, vol. 6, no. 2575.

*Senate Requested Supreme Judicial Court Opinion on the Bill to Create the Massachusetts Port Authority.* Massachusetts Legislative Documents: Senate, 1956, vol. 2, no. 704.

*Massachusetts Port Authority Annual Reports. 1960 - 1974.*

Rowland and MacNeal. *Port of Boston Waterborne Commerce Market and Development Requirements.* New York: 1964.

Arthur D. Little, Inc. *North Atlantic Port Survey: Report to the Boston Shipping Association.* Cambridge: 1966.

Federal Maritime Commission, Bureau of Domestic Regulation, Division of Terminals. *Staff Study of the Port of Boston.* Washington, D.C.: U.S. Government Printing Office, 1967.

Legislative Research Council. *Report Relative to the Promotion of the Port of Boston.* Massachusetts Legislative Documents: House, 1968, vol. 10, no. 4852.

Abt Associates, Inc. *The Boston Seaport, 1970 - 1990.* Cambridge: 1970.

Frederic R. Harris, Inc. *Feasibility Investigation: Massport Out-To-Sea Oil Terminal System,* Interim Report. Boston: 1970.

Hartman, Chester W., et al. *The Massachusetts Port Authority: Public Purpose and Public Accountability.* Cambridge: 1970.

U.S. Department of Commerce, Maritime Administration. *MarAd 1970 Year of Transition, Annual Report for Fiscal Year 1970.* Washington, D.C.: U.S. Government Printing Office, 1971.

Massachusetts Institute of Technology. *Economic Factors in the Development of a Coastal Zone.* Cambridge: M.I.T. Press, 1970.

Massachusetts Institute of Technology Report No. 21. *Project Bosporus, Boston Port Utilization Study.* Cambridge: M.I.T. Press, 1970.

Frederic R. Harris, Inc. *Feasibility Investigation: Massport Out-To-Sea Oil Terminal, Supplemental Report.* Boston: 1971.

Metropolitan Area Planning Council, *Boston Harbor Islands Comprehensive Plan.* Boston: 1972.

Newsome and Co., Inc. *Public Relations Study and Recommendations Prepared for the Massachusetts Port Authority.* Boston: 1972.

U.S. Department of Transportation, *Saint Lawrence Seaway Development Corporation 1972 Annual Report.* Washington, D.C.: U.S. Government Printing Office, 1973.

Hood, Edwin M. *Statement Before Committee on Merchant Marine and Fisheries,* House of Representatives. July 11, 1973.

C. E. Maguire Inc. *New Container Facilities for Massport: A Feasibility Study.* Waltham, Mass.: 1973.

Porricelli, Joseph D., and Virgil F. Keith. *Tankers and the U.S. Energy Situation—An Economic and Environmental Analysis.* Presented at the Intersociety Transportation Conference, Denver, Colorado, September 24–27, 1973.

Shoupp, William E. *World Energy and the Oceans.* Second Annual Sea Grant Lecture. Massachusetts Institute of Technology Sea Grant Program: Report No. MITSG 74-7, 1973.

U.S. Congress, House, Committee on Merchant Marine and Fisheries. *High Seas Oil Port Act.* Report 93 692 to Accompany H.R. 5898. 93rd Congress, 1st Session, 1973.

U.S. Congress, House, *Off Shore Ports and Terminals. Hearing Before the House Committee on Merchant Marine and Fisheries on H.R. 5090 and H.R. 5898.* 93rd Congress, 1st Session, 1973.

U.S. Department of Commerce, Maritime Administration. *Draft Environmental Impact Statement, Tanker Program.* Washington, D.C.: U.S. Government Printing Office, 1973.

U.S. Department of Commerce, Maritime Administration. *Pending Construction Differential Subsidy Applications.* Washington, D.C.: U.S. Government Printing Office, 1973.

Raytheon Company. *Massport Marine Deepwater Terminal Study, Site and Terminal Selection.* Bedford, Mass.: 1974.

**Legal Sources (chronological)**

*Federal*

Equalization of Rates of North Atlantic Ports. 311 Interstate Commerce Commission 689. 1959.

Boston & Maine Railroad vs. U.S. 202F. supp. 830. 1962.

Baltimore & Ohio Railroad vs. Boston & Maine Railroad. 373 U.S. 372. 1963.

*Massachusetts*

*An Act to Create Boards of Harbor and Land Commissioners.* Chapter 149 of the Massachusetts Acts and Resolves of 1877.

*An Act to Create a Board of Harbor and Land Commissioners.* Chapter 263 of the Massachusetts Acts and Resolves of 1879.

*An Act to Purchase Land in East Boston.* Chapter 648 of the Massachusetts Acts and Resolves of 1910.

*An Act Relevant to the Development of the Port of Boston.* Chapter 748 of the Massachusetts Acts and Resolves of 1911.

*An Act Relative to the Directors of the Port of Boston.* Chapter 712 of the Massachusetts Acts and Resolves of 1914.

*An Act to Create a Commission on Waterways and Public Lands.* Chapter 288 of the Massachusetts Acts and Resolves of 1916.

*An Act to Organize in Departments the Executive and Administrative Functions of the Commonwealth.* Chapter 350 of the Massachusetts Acts and Resolves of 1919.

*An Act Establishing the Boston Port Authority.* Chapter 229 of the Massachusetts Acts and Resolves of 1929.

*An Act Abolishing the Boston Port Authority and Establishing a Port of Boston Authority.* Chapter 619 of the Massachusetts Acts and Resolves of 1945.

*An Act Abolishing the Port of Boston Authority and Establishing the Port of Boston Commission.* Chapter 608 of the Massachusetts Acts and Resolves of 1953.

*Massachusetts General Laws Annotated. Massachusetts Port Authority.* C91, s 1-2.

*An Act Establishing the Massachusetts Port Authority.* Chapter 465 of the Massachusetts Acts and Resolves of 1956.

*An Act Establishing a Division of Environmental Protection Within the Department of the Attorney General, and Directing the Preparation of Environmental Impact Reports.* Chapter 781 of the Massachusetts Acts and Resolves of 1972.

## Newspapers (chronological)

"Rates Verdict to Spur Port, New England Railroads. *Boston Globe,* May 21, 1963, pp. 1, 13.

"Boston Shipping Association protests MPA $1 surcharge." *Boston Globe,* January 27, 1966, p. 5.

"Bins Closed—Boston Loses Grain Deal." *Boston Globe,* February 10, 1966, p. 3.

"BSA Charges Fly." *Boston Globe,* February 10, 1966, p. 3.

"MPA, New Role." *Boston Globe,* February 10, 1966, p. 1.

"Boston Port Decline Faces Quiz." *Christian Science Monitor,* March 28, 1967, p. 2.

"Boston Hasn't Halted Its Shipping Decline." *Christian Science Monitor,* March 31, 1967, p. 2.

"New Cargoes For Boston Harbor." *Christian Science Monitor,* May 6, 1967, p. 2.

"Will New Container Crane Revitalize Boston's Port." *Christian Science Monitor,* June 21, 1971, p. 4.

"Hub to Get $30m Terminal." *Boston Sunday Herald Traveler and Advertiser,* July 2, 1972, sec. 2, p. 24.

"Containers Crucial to Boston Shipping." *Boston Globe,* July 9, 1972, p. 25.

"Massport's Oil Project Labelled Contradictory by State Sen. Bulger." *Boston Globe,* October 6, 1972, p. 3.

"King Presses for Offshore Oil Terminal." *Boston Herald American,* November 12, 1973, p. 3.

"New England Public Oil Corporation Urged." *Christian Science Monitor,* December 5, 1973, p. 3.

"Bay State Congressmen back Massport Oil Terminal." *Boston Globe,* November 11, 1973, p. 17.

"Anatomy of a Fiasco." *Boston Herald America,* January 9, 1974, p. 1.

"Boston Expected to Continue Container and Cruise Gains." *Boston Globe,* January 13, 1974, p. A-10.

"Containing a Port Facility." *Boston Globe,* February 28, 1974, p. 18.

"Massport Curb Won by White." *Boston Globe,* March 14, 1974, p. 12.

Yudis, Anthony J. "Airport and Labor Top Lures in Bringing Business to Boston." *Boston Evening Globe,* March 15, 1974, p. 23.

"House Kills Bill Giving Sargent Control over Massport Spending." *Boston Globe,* March 27, 1974, p. 3.

Francis, Edward. "Steamship Lines May End Land Bridge." *Boston Sunday Herald Advertiser,* March 31, 1974, sec. 3, p. 58.

"Massport's Golden Egg." *Boston Herald American,* April 20, 1974, p. 8.

"Over the Years, Massport Has Made Friends, Enemies with Controversial Director." *Boston Globe,* November 22, 1974, p. 3.

"King Firing: A Month of Planning." *Boston Sunday Globe,* November 24, 1974, p. 1.

"Strike Isolates Boston, Shipper Says." *Boston Globe,* December 11, 1974, p. 4.

"Boston Container Terminal At Naval Annex Is Urged." *Boston Globe,* March 6, 1975, p. 19.

## Magazines and Journals (chronological)

Plotkin, Abe. "The Port and Parity: How Boston Got the 'Business'." *Boston,* vol. 55, no. 8, September 1963, pp. 50-61.

148

Hammond, James. "Problems That Plague the Port." *Boston,* vol. 60, no. 2, February 1968, pp. 45–48.

Hammond, James. "Perspective on the Port." *Boston,* vol. 59, no. 2, February 1967, pp. 51–54.

Hammond, James. "Soundings at the Port—High Tides Ahead." *Boston,* vol. 62, no. 2, February 1970, pp. 61–67.

Willingham, Mike. "Planning and Development of Port Facilities." *Ocean Industry,* August 1972, pp. 29–31.

Lupo, Alan. "The Monarch of Massport." *Boston,* vol. 62, no. 7, July 1973, pp. 31–81.

Kasputys, Joseph, and Young, Joe Bill. "Subsidies, Seed Money, and National Security." *Seapower,* September 1973, pp. 23–30.

Zannetos, Zenon S. "Persistent Economic Misconceptions in the Transportation of Oil by Sea." *Maritime Studies and Management,* vol. 1, no. 2, October 1973.

Saunders, George D. "Land Bridge Comes of Age." *U.S. Naval Institute Proceedings,* December 1973, pp. 39–43.

"U.S. Shipbuilding Report." *Marine Engineering/Log,* February 1974, pp. 72–74.

Merton, Andy, "Why Slow and Steady Can't Lose in '74." *Boston,* vol. 66, no 3, March 1974, pp. 38–77.

Davis, Charles F. "Ship Industry Reports Inland Export Cargoes Backed Up." *Journal of Commerce,* March 6, 1974, p. 1.

"New England's Dilemma." *Time,* April 1974, p. 50.

Sansone, Wallace P. "Domestic Shipping and American Maritime Policy." U.S. Naval Institute Proceedings, Naval Review, 1974, pp. 164–177.

"Spills Decline." *Industry,* February 1975, p. 31.

## Other Sources (chronological)

President Nixon's Energy Message to the U.S. Congress, April 18, 1973.

McGlennon, John A.S., Regional Administrator, Environmental Protection Agency. Letter to Honorable Robert H. Quinn, Attorney General, Commonwealth of Massachusetts. August 2, 1973.

Geary, John J., Assistant Director, Piggyback and Containers Services, Boston & Maine Corporation. Interview held during Seminar on Surface Transportation, Containerization, and the Port of Boston. Sponsored by the International Center of New England, March 14, 1974.

Sweeney, Richard, and Moriconi, Rino, Massport Maritime Division Staff. Interviews March, 1975.

# Index

# Index

## About the Author

**Louis E. Cellineri** received the B.A. from Harvard College in 1967. He subsequently served in the U.S. Merchant Marine and spent several years with the Massachusetts Attorney General's Division of Environmental Protection, where he specialized in marine pollution. He received a Masters of Marine Affairs degree from the University of Rhode Island in 1974 and is currently employed by the National Oceanic and Atmospheric Administration in Washington, D.C.